Warm Smiles and Encouraging Words

Best Wishes

Wayne Brady

Wayne Brady

ON THE COVER

A self-portrait of the artist, Gary Brady II, and the author, his dad.

Referring to this drawing that reflects an incident from more than thirty years earlier when young Gary was playing youth football, I recently asked, "What do you think I was saying to you?"

Gary responded, "I don't remember what you were saying, but I know it was encouraging."

My heart melted and I knew as I completed this manuscript, this cover defines the heart from which I write.

DEDICATION

I dedicate this work to God and to my children.

Amazing Grace is what God had when He revealed Jesus Christ, His Son, to me. It was like I was dying, and He reached into my chest and massaged my cold dead heart with His own hands, occasionally jolting it with a touch from His Holy Spirit to keep it functioning properly.

My dilemma was that God poured His perfect love into an imperfect vessel. He knew I was not equipped to be a father, so He gave me children who are such a wonderful mix of love, talent, and personality to force me into the role.

My prayer today is that my children know beyond a shadow of doubt that my love for them is without end, and there are no strings attached.

I Love You Tammi, Terri, and Gary and no one can take that away!

Daddy

CONTENTS

INTRODUCTION

*Let everything you say be good
and helpful, so that your words
will be an encouragement to those
who hear them.* (Ephesians 4:29b
NLT)

I smile a lot. That doesn't mean I am free from pain
and worries. No, far from it. I seldom share my
issues in life with the outside world. However, in this
collection of stories, I have exposed my soul to lift
the reader. All are as free from political opinion as I
can make them.

I grew up around people who smiled a lot, people
who made jokes, people who kidded, people who
cared about each other, and people who wanted to see
others smile. I may have been naïve, but I felt warmth
from those who smiled at me and said encouraging
words to me, or who spoke positive things about me.

By the same token, I became very insecure around
people who seldom smiled, who always had
something negative to say about others, or who
complained about everything, often their complaint

centering around me or what I had done. I developed some deep insecure feelings and learned to try and overcome them by being more cruel than what I had received. I became very good at being unkind, but I was wrong.

God delivered me and now I want to heal rather than win. It feels so good to receive a broad smile followed by kind words. I figure I am not alone.

The stories in this book are written with the reader in mind. The first story is to set the tone for how God has encouraged me throughout my life. After that, I have included stories to offer you hope, some to inspire you to be a light for others, a section to encourage you to keep growing, a few to remind you of the simple joy of life, and finally a short teaching on writing to encourage you to record your thoughts and ideas to share with others.

As you read through this book, feel free to write your remembrances, thoughts, or ideas under the NOTES sections after many of the stories. Let your notes spark memories of events and people from your life.

I Pray God's Blessings on all who read these stories.

NOTES

CHICKEN LITTLE & THE MONEY TREE

I was grocery shopping the other day when a stranger said to me, "You have a warm and friendly smile."

"Thank you, it's people like you who make it easy for me to keep smiling," I responded.

As I walked away, my mind traveled back nearly fifty years to a substitute grandfather I had when I was growing up. The thing I remember most about him was his warm friendly smile.

The second to the oldest of my mother's seven brothers, his only child, a daughter, had married and moved away with her military husband. I came along at the perfect time to fill a void in his life. I became a primary beneficiary of a tremendous amount of love that Uncle Levi and Aunt Evie had to give.

He called me Chicken Little after an incident at the home of another of my mother's brothers. In those days, they allowed chickens to wander around the yard like they were pets. Uncle Ward had a yard full of them. One day while walking around the yard, I got too close to one of his banty roosters. The feisty little chicken attacked me and chased me around the yard. Uncle Ward picked me up as I excitedly told him about the "Chicken Little" running me around the yard. They picked up on it and began calling me Chicken Little.

Some of my earliest memories include visiting Uncle Levi's turn-of–the-century home located on the edge of the small town of Shubuta, Mississippi, and picking up pecans that had fallen from the huge trees in his front yard. Sometimes, we would go down to his peanut patch, and pull fresh green peanuts from his garden. Although he allowed me to eat a few raw peanuts, he would make me wait until he boiled them in saltwater before I could eat my fill of them.

My most precious thoughts of Uncle Levi are how he went to great effort to perpetuate a ruse on a small child, rivaled only by Santa Claus at Christmas. He told me he had a "special" tree in his yard and there were no others like it in the world. To make it even more special, he told everyone I was the only person he allowed to pick its fruit. The details of what the tree looked like have almost completely faded from my memory, but the idea will be with me until I die.

I don't know how he did it, but on the days that the fruit was ready to be harvested, Uncle Levi would meet me as I got out of my parents' car, lift me in his arms, and carry me to the rear of his home. There it stood, in the middle of a hedgerow. A magnificent tree completely covered with its fantastic fruit. I have never seen another like it, and I alone could pick from it.

Uncle Levi would carry me over and hold me high enough to pick the fruit from the upper branches before lowering me to the ground to complete the harvest.

Then he would back off, beaming with pleasure as I excitedly pulled the apples, oranges, peaches, pears, dollar bills, and sparkling new coins from the tree.

My brother told me the reason I was the only one allowed to pick from it was because I was the only one naïve enough to believe the tree was real. I prefer to imagine how happy it must have made Uncle Levi to see the excitement of a child's Innocency, accepting what he sees as real.

I cannot eat boiled peanuts today without remembering the person who meant so much to me when I was so impressionable. I know the comfort that I feel every time I think about the effort he must have put into making my life a little more special.

Uncle Levi was instrumental in many ways to my maturation from a child to manhood. He was a deacon in the church, and I learned to sing with joy sitting on a pew beside him. When I was fourteen, he allowed me to take the wheel of his most prized possession, a 1948 Ford Deluxe. We would drive those graveled roads, stopping often to visit friends and relatives. In those visits, I experienced the joy and pleasure that he brought to everyone, and more importantly, I learned the value of a warm friendly smile.

My wife met Uncle Levi briefly in the hospital just a few days before he died. To this day she remembers how happy he was to see us, and how happy he was that I was lucky enough to have a wife like her, a wife who would cook biscuits for a little boy who loved them.

I hope that I offer a smile of joy and acceptance to others, a little like Uncle Levi.

NOTES

HOPE

S tories to remind you how crucial you are to this world, to your family, to your friends, to me, and to God.

You are Important

Have you ever felt worthless, insignificant, or of little value? It is a product of our environment and attacks many of us from time-to-time.

Years ago, I learned a simple test to determine if people were listening. I would stop talking in the middle of a thought or an idea. If no one asked me to continue, I decided that they were either not paying attention, or they were glad I stopped.

The test worked pretty-well and fostered my feelings of rejection. I learned to shut my mouth more and more often. Mistakenly, I concluded that no one was interested in anything I had to say.

I was wrong! There are some who appreciate me and value my opinion. I share for them. The challenge is when to stop talking. Talk should be balanced with a lot of listening.

As a child, I learned the value of listening, especially to adults.

When her children and their families gathered at my grandmother's house and the tales started, children listened. The stories were entertaining; some were obvious exaggerations, a few were educational, but all were worth hearing. From the most talented to the least, they all had something of value to share.

My grandmother never lived in a house with an indoor toilet. She spoke Mississippi country and wrote like a sixth grader, but she was as wise as King Solomon. Ms. Hattie's wisdom grew rapidly when my grandfather passed away and left her with nine children. It took another leap when Uncle Sam sent six of her boys half-way around the world to fight against other mother's sons who were conscripted in Japan's and Hitler's misguided attempts to conquer the world.

She overcame through prayer, studying God's Word, hearing sound doctrine, and applying it in her life. When she spoke, I listened.

Back to you and me. Are we important? Absolutely! We have gained an incredible amount of wisdom through our life experiences. The longer we live, the more resilient we become. With every experience, we grow a little wiser, and when we ask God for His help, we grow even faster.

God tells us, "If you need wisdom, ask our generous God, and He will give it to you. He will not rebuke you for asking." (James 1:5 NLT)

There are so many who want and need to learn what we know. Please share yourself; it is how God works through us.

I Pray God's Blessings on You.

NOTES

One of a Kind

Heaven is not a place for clones. God doesn't want us to be exactly like anyone else.

Occasionally, I wonder what heaven will be like. Will there literally be streets paved with gold? Will we float around like angels? Will we all look alike? Will we all act alike? Will we all stand around a throne praising God in some-kind-of-a-choreographed ritual?

Before I continue, I must qualify my writing with a disclaimer, "I am not a theologian." However, I do believe God speaks to me, and sometimes I hear His voice, turn to give Him my full attention, and listen to what He is saying. This is one of those times.

I do not know what we will be doing in heaven, but there is no reason for any of us to be there if we all are identical. What value would one be versus another if there are no differences?

I believe God wants us to be us.

God mixed the ingredients for our mind, body and soul differently for each of us. Then he let His process work in us to cause us to be completely different from any other person. He created us to be unique, only one of a kind. Why? Because He wants fellowship with each of us on a personal basis.

If we were exactly alike, He would only need one of us. God would not be satisfied if every person worshipped Him out of something other than our Love for Him. That is why He spends a lifetime developing us into the people we eventually become.

When God calls you home, He wants YOU, not anyone else. I am glad He knows me.

NOTES

God Knows You

While lying in bed this morning, I spoke to God like I normally do, as I would to a best friend. In a soft calm voice, I said, "I am sorry Father for being the way I am and causing so many misunderstandings. I really don't want to be this way."

At that point, He interrupted and responded, "Don't apologize for who you are. That is a reflection on Me and what I have done for you. Are you perfect? In your eyes, no. Am I satisfied with you? Yes."

Then He said, "Take some time to think on My comments and always remember that I adopted you. I came to you, and I love you. No matter what you think, you are My child forever. Now, share with others."

Wow, the most powerful Being in all of forever talking to me, a simple man from a simple place during a simple time. Why would He do that? It is simple. There are more of us than there are of perfect people. In fact, there are no perfect people.

We are all the result of our own God instilled personalities, a product of our environment, and a mixture of every encounter we have had with others throughout our lives.

The way I interpret God's Words to me is that I am to always be mindful of Him. He is always there encouraging me, forever rooting for me, and constantly bragging on me.

All we need to do to better understand this is to think about our own children or other significant people in our lives (mother, father, brothers, sisters, special friends, etc.). No matter how imperfect they are, they are always 100% acceptable to us.

I am not saying this to allow us an excuse to do anything we want. We are to listen to God and others who care for us without reservation and be aware when we need to do some things better. Just like a good friend, God is patient and forgiving, and always has our best interests at heart.

Father, I ask that You continue to deal with me, that You never give up on me, and that You never give up on anyone who reads these words. I don't know why You are the way You are, but I am thankful that You are. I Love You in Jesus' name.

NOTES

Excited to See You

I get excited when I see you.

My wife, Carolyn, and I left home early one morning headed across the bay to run some errands, which we decided would include breakfast somewhere special. Just a few blocks from home, I noticed a dark SUV approaching from a side street. It caught Carolyn off guard as I started frantically blowing the horn. No, the car was not pulling into our path. I was blowing to get the driver's attention.

It took Carolyn a second to realize that it was Terri, our daughter, but then she started waving also. I told Carolyn, "You better get your phone out of your purse." Sure enough, in a few seconds her phone started ringing.

Oh, the sweetness when we see someone we love in an unexpected setting.

My dad has been gone more than three decades, but I can still remember the warm feeling I got when I would be driving some place, look up, and there he was. I cherish the wonderful memory of when he would walk in from work, smile at me, hand me his lunch box after a hard day's work, and flood my childhood heart with joy.

I have experienced countless times of joy from seeing a grandchild, a son, a daughter, or a friend in some place I didn't expect.

My heart surges with heightened energy when I walk into a place, and someone who recognizes me says, "Well, if it isn't Wayne Brady," or "Hey, Wayne, come over here and let me introduce you to someone," or any other happy-face greeting.

What do you think? For me the joy is because someone recognizes me, likes me, and is glad to express their pleasure to me. No matter my current situation, my face can't hold back a smile any time someone offers a warm greeting to me.

Case in point, Bryant-Denny Stadium last Saturday preparing for the University of Alabama versus Mississippi State football game. I am climbing the steps to the row where my seat is, and I hear a voice, "Hey, Wayne."

I look up and a man several rows higher up is frantically waving with a big ole smile on his face. I don't immediately recognize him. I don't turn to go down my aisle, choosing instead to go and talk with this person. When I reach the man, we carry on a short conversation before I admit to him, "Please forgive me, but I don't remember your name." He introduces himself, and I tell him my name is Wayne Brady.

He says to me, "You look like Ward, a friend I have known for years."

We exchange a few more pleasantries, I smile and say, "It is good to meet you," turn and head to my seat. I now have a new friend in Tuscaloosa on game day.

All of this said, I am just as happy if I see you, even if you don't see me and return the smile. It is you who excites me.

I am so thankful for all of you who have been a part of my life; you are my joy. God Bless You.

NOTES

Expect Good Things

As I have already said, I am not a theologian and I don't intend for what follows to lead to a deep spiritual discussion. My words simply describe how God revealed Himself to me again this morning as I started typing words into my computer.

I am so thankful I live in the dispensation of Jesus Christ. What does that mean? I thought I knew, but this morning God opened my mind and poured in a little different understanding.

When I moved the cursor over the word "dispensation" in the preceding paragraph and hit <shift F7>, several synonyms popped up that immediately touched my heart:

1) Special consideration
2) Privilege
3) Relaxation of the rules
4) Exemption

I expect good things to happen to me, not because I am anyone of significance in the world. No, God just put into me a servant's heart. I like to help people. If I see a need, often, I see a solution. Naturally, I want to resolve it. I don't see every need, I don't always have an answer, and sometimes I know to just stay out of certain situations.

Having a servant's heart, I believe God brings me in contact with others who also have a heart toward people. Most of the time when I go to someone for help with a problem, I get the perfect person to resolve it. Occasionally, I get a grouch. Many times, I can alter the disposition of someone who is having a bad day with a few kind words; sometimes not.

Often, I seem to get special consideration. Why do I receive special privileges? Why would someone relax rules for me? Why am I exempted from some laws? Why do I always expect good things to happen to me?

I believe it is because of a scriptural principle that most of us learned when we were children: The Golden Rule – "Do unto others as you would have them do unto you."

Jesus Christ was the first to say it, "Therefore all things whatsoever ye would that men should do to you, do ye even so to them: for this is the law and the prophets." (Matthew 7:12 KJV)

All I am saying is, if we treat others with kindness, we are likely to be treated kindly. Over and over again, I find out that God has already put a sweet spirit into someone He knows I am about to need.

I hope you have had similar experiences. If you haven't noticed in the past, start looking, and realize how God paves the roads we are about to travel.

NOTES

Expect Good Things Too

This is a follow-up to the previous article. In it I stated, "I expect good things to happen to me."

Is everything good that happens to me? Does everyone treat me kindly? The obvious answer to both is, no. However, the words of the Psalmist, "Surely goodness and mercy shall follow me all the days of my life:" (Psalms 23:6 KJV) are apparent in my life.

When did I first notice that I was receiving special consideration? I believe it was when I was a boy. A few people treated me special enough to make me realize there are a lot of good people in this world, and most of them want to treat others well.

Who were these extraordinary people? The first one who comes to mind is my daddy. He always had time for me and was always there with good advice for me to live by. There were just too many instances to start naming them here.

Both of my grandfathers passed away ten years before I was born, so my mother's seven brothers filled those roles. These men treated me like I was important; each in his own unique way. Several took me to church and introduced me to Christian people. Others allowed me to drive them to local bootleggers' houses. Mississippi was "dry" at that time, and you couldn't buy liquor legally anywhere in the state.

The people I met in both places, church and at the bootleggers, were principled, respectful, friendly, outgoing, and they all taught good ole Mississippi values. I never felt uncomfortable or threatened in either place because adults protected children.

My list could go on to include relatives on both sides of the family, and then extend to friends growing up. What can I say about my friends?

When I was four-years old, we moved into a government housing project that was chock-full of children. The war was over, soldiers were home, jobs were available, and the first wave of baby boomers was eager to explore the world on the other side of those screen doors. We were off and running. With hundreds of children to play with, there were more than enough who became good friends. I am still close with some after more than sixty, fifty, or forty years.

Thinking back, being a part of those who God allowed in my life molded me into the person I am today. I know my faults and I am working to correct some of them, but if you want to be my friend, accept me "as is" and I will be yours for life.

My prayer today is that God will send people into your life who help you feel as special as you are, and in turn, you help others realize, they too, are important.

Need a Friend? God Will Provide

Have you ever had the *mully-grubs? I have. One day when I had a particularly bad case, I said to God, "I need a friend." I was feeling pretty sorry for myself and I thought, *everyone I know appears to have more than enough people in their lives and probably don't have time for anyone else.*

I sat for a little while wondering to myself, *how is He going to do it? I don't go places to meet new people, and everyone I meet seems to already be too busy to have time for me.*

Did God answer my simple prayer? You bet. He didn't bring a line-up of people into my presence and say, "Choose some friends from this group."

God spoke simply to me, "If you want to have a friend, you have to be a friend."

As I reflect back, God allowed me to just keep going and doing the thing I loved most; meeting people.

It has been amazing to watch how people have come into my life. In many cases, God showed me a person with a need (most of the time a minor one) and then nudged me to check on them. God reminded me of friends from the past who were in similar situations and encouraged me to call them. I learned that most of the time people only want a friendly face and an offer to pray with them.

I soon realized that I was no longer friendless and that I never was. Often, I just needed to make the first contact.

I learned a valuable lesson on friendship from Carter Bryars, a longtime friend. He sold industrial equipment in the Mobile area and was very good at it. I used some of the equipment he sold, but I was a little afraid of meeting him because one friend told me, "He is a super salesman." I didn't know if I could resist buying things I didn't need from a real pro.

Then one day I met him, and he was not like I imagined at all. He was friendly, outgoing, and talked almost non-stop, but he never asked me to buy anything. He did tell me the types of things he sold and offered to help me anytime I needed something. He never bragged, but he let me know that he started with Gulf Coast Marine right out of high school and except for a few years fighting during World War II (he charged the beaches of Normandy on D-Day); he worked there his entire life.

He checked in with me regularly. He always asked about any problems I may be having and continued to offer to help me. When I finally called him and asked for help, he told me that he could not sell the product I needed for geographical reasons within their distribution. That didn't matter to him; he worked like he was going to make a fortune off my one little order that would go to his competitor. He was always like that, and over the years I wound up buying a lot of stuff from his company because I could, and I wanted to.

Carter lived a long full life and has gone on to be with The Lord. He told me once, "I never asked a friend for his business, but every person I ever did business with became my friend." What a legacy.

I am grateful for each and every person in my life, and especially for those who have become my friends, because our children and grandchildren are getting busier, and have other activities and people they are spending time with.

Do I have all the friends I need? No way, and if you would like to be my friend just reach out to me.

*Definition: mully-grubs - *A period of time when one is feeling down and out. Depressed, hopeless, lonely and sad.* - From the Urban Dictionary

NOTES

Success

I declare I am a product of the Most-High God's loving kindness for one of His own.

Some may look at me and say, "He is not such a much." Seeing what others have accomplished; my success is minuscule.

The fact is that even though I don't deserve more than the next person, my wonderful Father keeps opening doors for me.

I am not a so called "Name it and Claim it" Christian but I do expect people to be good to me and for good things to happen to me. Does it always happen? No. Sometimes people treat me really bad. I just tend to not focus on those.

It is amazing how you feel when you walk into a business or a room full of people expecting a smile or positive feedback. That attitude causes me to smile and be nice, most of the time, which helps set the tone for an encounter.

I like receiving smiles which helps me be openly friendly to start a conversation.

What are some of the keys to my life of joy?

1. Positive attitude: I am just hardheaded enough to believe things are going to get better, at least by the next time.

2. Good work habits: My daddy taught me to work, to do it right, and to do a little extra so you will feel good about what you do. On the job, never look as if you were, "Shot out of a canon at quitting time." Don't ever be the first person out of the door.

3. Willing to learn: Always! We never get too old to learn. We may have difficulty learning some things, but we should keep up with technology. We should always be looking for something different to try. Who knows? We may really enjoy it.

4. Take responsibility for my own success or failure. If I work hard, study long, and be personable with everyone I meet, the odds for success tend to move in my favor. On the other hand, if I am lazy, derelict in my duties, or only do the minimum to get by; I only have myself to blame for the lack of success in my life.

5. Trust in something bigger than yourself. You are not the biggest component of your life. There is a God who loves you, His creation. He will open doors, He will lead you, and He will direct you to make good decisions. He has for so many others. Why not you?

As Stuart Hamblen so eloquently immortalized after he realized the touch of the Master's hand:

It is no secret what God can do
What He's done for others, He'll do for you
With arms wide open, He'll pardon you
It is no secret what God can do

NOTES

Pinball of Life

H ave you ever felt like a pinball?
What's a pinball?
I am glad you asked.

A pinball lives in a small world under glass, protected from the elements but driven by outside forces beyond its control.

A person drops a coin into a pinball machine, a ball rolls into the launch chute, and when he is ready, the player releases a mechanism that catapults the dormant pinball to life. From this point until its life cycle is over, points are added every time the ball encounters an obstacle. The goal is to keep the ball alive by repeatedly slamming it back to life every time it approaches a final resting place, ultimately earning more points than other players.

In 1963, life was good for me. What more could I ask for during my senior year of high school? A friend and classmate introduced me to the owner of Tom's Dairy Freeze. Tom Harris, a friend to all the young people who knew him, became my friend and hired me for the perfect job.

Dinner, the three nights-a-week I worked, consisted of a hamburger, an order of French fries, a coke, and some of Tom's homemade ice cream for dessert before my shift was over. I earned a huge salary; 70¢ per hour, worked lots of hours, 20 per week, and had plenty of spending money. What could a seventeen-year-old do with $14 a week?

I lived at home and ate as many meals as I wanted there; I just had to be there when they were served. Mother cooked good ole country meals like fried chicken or pork chops, fresh vegetables, corn bread, sweet tea, and occasionally a dessert.

I was living a teenager's perfect life. With the car my daddy bought for me to drive, $14 was enough to put gas in the tank, take a girl to a movie, and every once in a while, have some left to buy beer. Yeah, we teenagers could and would get it, and drink it.

Life for me was much easier than for many of my peers.

But I have veered off subject. There was a pin-ball machine in Tom's. This machine was way before computerized games, but it still commanded a lot of attention. Many local young men—ages 20 to 35— dropped case dimes, one after another, into that machine. They all wanted to be the champion. No matter how hard they tried, very few could consistently beat Tom who was the most successful player over the long haul. I suspect he spent a lot of afternoons after the lunch rush, before school was dismissed, honing his skills.

Life Lesson:

Back to my first question, "Have you ever felt like a pinball?"

Life sometimes treats us as if we are a pinball. Just as soon as we overcome one problem, we immediately encounter another. Occasionally, we roll into a slow period with little conflict, almost lulled into complacency, and then almost violently some external force thrusts us back into the world of reality.

It is how we deal with each obstacle of life that defines us.

I pray that God reveals Himself clearly to you through each life experience, and that you become bolder in your walk of faith.

The Lord Bless and Keep You Today.

<u>NOTES</u>

Feel Like Giving Up—Don't

Do you ever feel overwhelmed? Are there days when you could just give up? Do you see obstacles that stand in the way of your success? Even though failure may appear imminent, some of the difficulty may be designed to strengthen you.

I am not trained or qualified in the field of psychiatry, and I am very limited in my understanding of how the human mind and body functions. This entire article is based strictly on my limited appreciation for how God destined us to succeed. Failure should not be an option for any of us.

God left us the following instructions, "And be not conformed to this world: but be ye transformed by the renewing of your mind, that ye may prove what is that good, and acceptable, and perfect, will of God." (Romans 12:2 KJV)

How do we renew our mind? It is not as hard or as spiritual as we may initially think.

I am not and have never been a physically talented or active person. In high school I hated exercising and avoided it as much as possible. It was no surprise that just three years after my last high school physical education class, I was overweight and out of shape.

That was bad enough, but I was on my way to Fort Leonard Wood, Missouri, to undergo basic training for the United States Army Reserve.

It was not a pleasant experience. If not for a lot of men who encouraged me every step of the way, I would not have made it.

During a particularly challenging session, one of the drill sergeants said to us, "Men, I know that this is difficult and at times you may think you are going to die if you take one more step. I promise, you won't die. You will make it through. In a very short time after you leave here, your brain will push the remembrance of the misery you are going through now right out. You may remember that you were miserable here, but you won't be able to recall the exact feelings."

That sergeant was right then, and he is right now. I quickly forgot the near failure on my part, and remembered mostly the men who encouraged me daily to keep going.

In life we can't help getting into some difficult situations, but when we come out of those circumstances, God put within us the ability to forget the misery and remember those who helped us make it through.

The human brain is a wonderful part of our body, designed by God to provide us with unique abilities based on information it receives from our five senses (sight, hearing, taste, smell, and touch).

The brain controls our body temperature, blood pressure, heart rate, and breathing. It gives us our ability to reason, imagine, and speak the appropriate word or exclamation at exactly the right moment. It controls all of our movements required to walk, talk, stand, or sit.

However, I believe one important function of our brain is to know when to let something go. It knows that many memories would only serve to hurt us further, or hold us back and prevent us from reaching for the dreams instilled in us by our Creator. Yes, our brain has the ability to hide certain information, much of it negative, and push it out of our minds in order to make room for thoughts that encourage us.

I realize that many of us are burdened with some unhealthy experiences in life. With very little effort on our part, painful memories can overwhelm us and tempt us to give up, consuming our faith in the process. We have to remind ourselves of the hope God has put within us, find people who encourage us to pursue our own dreams, and minimize input from those who would discourage us.

"Finally, brethren, whatsoever things are true, whatsoever things are honest, whatsoever things are just, whatsoever things are pure, whatsoever things are lovely, whatsoever things are of good report; if there be any virtue, and if there be any praise, think on these things." (Philippians 4:8 KJV)

NOTES

Things to know about Christians

With politicians and others giving their view of what a Christian should be, may I have a turn? Having lived nearly two-thirds of my life as a Christian, I have learned a few things.

First, when a person accepts Jesus Christ as savior, that person becomes a Christian.

Even as a Christian, it is impossible to live perfectly. Although we want to do God's will, often we fail.

Worse yet, occasionally we completely ignore God's teachings.

We go to church, listen to preaching, read the Bible, pray, and open our hearts to receive from God.

We are taught to take care of our own and to treat others kindly.

We become devoted spouses, better fathers, more loving mothers, responsible children, helpful neighbors, and honest business associates.

We seek forgiveness as we learn to forgive.

We are many, at distinct levels of maturity and experience.

We are one, with a free will to read and interpret the Bible for ourselves.

We try to be honest with God. We take responsibility for our actions.

Although we love life, we know there is more.

One day we will trade time for eternity and be reunited with those who have gone before us in a place God has prepared for us.

Even with our faults, when we meet Him face-to-face, I believe God will open His arms and welcome us, saying, "Come in. I am so glad to see you."

First published in the Press-Register, the newspaper for Mobile, Alabama January 20, 2010

NOTES

A Life Worth Living

One day removed from the loss of Ivan, I still hurt. I knew it was going to be bad but not this bad.

My trusted friend followed my lead and did everything that I asked. I doubt he suspected anything different this day. He had no reason to believe this visit to the vet would be any different than earlier trips.

The doctor was clear. Finding a vein was the only difficult part. Given that, death would come quickly.

After a few minutes alone with Ivan, we called the doctor in.

Ivan was docile when we lifted him onto the cold stainless table. The doctor's assistant hugged his head and Carolyn and I rubbed him gently. It didn't take much probing for the doctor's expert hand to find a vein. I guess it was habit that caused the doctor to wipe the entry point with an alcohol filled cotton ball.

Dr. Wesson's hand was ever so steady as he guided the tiny needle into Ivan's paw. In an instant, he pressed the translucent plunger forcing the blood-red liquid into Ivan's system.

Death came quickly, too quickly. In just a few seconds, Ivan's eyes closed, his tongue eased out, and he was gone. Dr. Wesson checked for a heartbeat and confirmed that life had gone out of him. I could no longer hold back.

The tears flowed fast and furious. Carolyn and I just stood holding him, holding each other, and questioning whether or not we had done the right thing. I am not sure that we will ever know that.

The one thing that I do know is that Ivan was the best. We were as good to him as we could be, and this was one of the hardest things that I have ever had to do.

Good-bye Ivan. I am sorry it had to end this way. I don't know how you felt but I do know the tremendous pain that I have; the loneliness, the hurt, and the guilt. I wouldn't do anything to make any of it go away if it meant that I would have never known you.

Good-bye Ivan, I hope to see you again.

Weeks later!

I walk into the house and expect Ivan to appear, his tail wagging back and forth like a pendulum in high gear. His cold wet nose nudging for some response. No, he doesn't come. No, I am alone, the worst thing that can happen to anyone.

God programmed us for fellowship and love. Fellowship and love between people, or between people and their beloved pets. Maybe one day we will consider another dog, just not today. Maybe one day.

Authors Note: *Our son, Gary, brought this wonderful animal into our life and left him in our care for most of the time, even to the end.*

NOTES

I Love my Country

What's right in our world?

I was reminded how great our country is when my wife and I attended a naturalization ceremony last Friday, November 13th in the year of our Lord 2015, at the Naval Aviation Museum in Pensacola, Florida. We were there to witness a friend complete the naturalization process.

U.S. District Judge M. Casey Rodgers presided over the transformation process from immigrant to U. S. Citizen for seventy-two eager individuals.

After the initial presentation of the flag with the accompanying national anthem, two fifth-grade students, Ryan Seaton and Olivia Mead, from Liza Jackson Preparatory School presented their winning essays on the topic "Why I'm glad America is a nation of immigrants."

Wow, I am impressed at the depth of understanding these two children exhibited for our country, and the importance for us to allow others to experience what we have.

Judge Rodgers led us through the naturalization process, like one would weave fine linen to clothe a newborn infant for presentation to the world. She conducted a well-orchestrated program which included the presentation of the candidates, their swearing in, and their declaration of citizenship.

Each new citizen demonstrated their understanding of, and their ability for speaking English, by introducing themselves and telling us their country of origin.

Afterward, Judge Rodgers asked the audience to join in as the entire fifth grade class led the new citizens through the honor of reciting their first "Pledge of Allegiance," and then the singing of "The National Anthem" as full-fledged Americans.

The keynote speaker, Captain Keith Hoskins, commanding officer of the Pensacola Naval Air Station, eloquently reminded us of some of our rights; The protection of our faith, the pursuit of happiness, and freedom of speech. He stressed to us the importance of revering our veterans, noting that six of the new citizens are already serving in our armed services, and reminded us that many have made the ultimate sacrifice to maintain the freedoms we enjoy. Then he encouraged the new citizens to get involved, to participate in our government, to be of service to our country, and to be of service to others.

Captain Hoskins dissected the pledge the new citizens had just recited, highlighted the meaning of this sacred vow, and then reminded us to count it a tremendous privilege to sing the immortal words of Francis Scott Key, our National Anthem, with an emphasis on the final verse, "O say does that star-spangled banner yet wave O'er the land of the free and the home of the brave?"

For the finale, Dr. Leo Day, a former minister of music at Olive Baptist Church in Pensacola, placed the icing on the cake when he completed the service, singing "America the Beautiful" in English as well as four other languages, representing some of the countries of origin of the new citizens.

As the service closed, Judge Rodgers reminded the new citizens that there was someone there to register them to vote.

This was a wonderful opportunity for my wife and me to privately renew our commitment to our nation, while watching these new citizens, representing dozens of countries dedicate themselves to the service of their new country.

This is what we are about.

GOD BLESS THE USA!

NOTES

INSPIRATION

S tories in this section are to inspire you to press
on, to remember how important you are, and to
be an inspiration for others.

Time Well Spent

Some may not realize just how much we pay to make, keep, and maintain relationships. I have been thinking about it, and I have recognized that there is a real cost associated with being a friend.

Cost, what cost? It's called time! We spend varying amounts of it in the many relationships we have.

In addition to talent and ability, each of us is given an amount of time to use during our lifetime. My grandmother spoke of seventy years being the standard for life, any more than that meant we were living on borrowed time. She died shortly after her seventieth birthday. In her mind, if she were still living, I would have already borrowed more than three years of extra time from someone who had their life shortened. I don't know how much more time that my credit-life line will allow for me to borrow, but I hope it's a lot. I wonder, "What is my credit rating?"

Two songs that offer differing perspectives on the use of time are, Jimmy Buffett's *Margaritaville* and Brad Paisley's *Time Well Wasted.*

I make no judgement, nor do I purport to understand the full meaning of either song. The first, with the popular theme, "Wastin' away again in Margaritaville," hints at allowing our mind to be clouded with alcohol and pointless activities. The second, declares there is value in wasting time. The words tell us that spending time with certain others is good, especially when we set aside some of those things that tend to rule our lives so we can interact with people who are important to us. In fact, Paisley proclaims that there is such a thing as, "Time Well Wasted."

I believe that the crucial thing for each of us is that we spend our time wisely.

I declare that every second I am with my wife, Carolyn, is time well spent. We each enhance and improve the other's life. We are better people for every moment we are together.

Some thoughts to ponder:

Occasionally, we may spend money frivolously until we realize that if we do not quit doing it, there won't be enough remaining to pay for the things we really want. We must control our spending to ensure that we have enough to go around.

Time is the same way. If we use it unwisely doing things that do not need to be done at that point in life, we may not have enough time to complete the things we want to do. Time is finite. Meaning for each of us, time is a set quantity that will end.

From millionaires to paupers, the amount of money we have is different for each of us. Likewise, the amount of time we have varies widely. How we use it is what makes our life move back and forth between wonderful and less than satisfactory.

Time: We give it, or we withhold it. I like giving time to things and people I love. Who or what did I spend my time for today? I attended church, heard a sermon on how to improve my life, and had lunch with friends. A good value for the time I expended.

I like being nice to people, a good value for the time I spend with them.

Hateful speaking or putting people down is a perfect example of wasting time.

Do you waste much of your time complaining about politicians or people who do not believe like you?

When I think about it, I am saddened by how much time I have spent foolishly. I would rather believe that I have been a perfect steward of my time. The only thing I can hope for is that I learned something of value during those time-wasting periods.

Is your time well spent, well wasted, or just wasted?

NOTES

A Time to Bloom

We have a plant in our back yard that appears to have only a single redeeming quality, it remains green year-round, but not a pretty shade of green, a green that is spotted with brown specs often with holes in the leaves. In other words, it lives most of its life looking as if it is dying. Nothing about the plant draws your attention to it.

One might ask, "Why would you cultivate such a scrawny plant? Why would you give it a place of prominence among your other plants? It certainly is not pretty in any way."

First, it does not require much nurturing or care, just a little water every now and then.

Second, is because of its unique growth cycle. Twice a year, tiny blooms begin growing around the edge of the leaves. Even as these blooms develop, the plant is still not much to look at.

Then one day, you step outside and realize that this less than beautiful plant is emitting a faint sweet aroma like the fragrance of honeysuckle. The drab looking blooms have come to life. They have turned up, stand erect, and appear ready to explode into full flower.

"Tomorrow," you say to yourself.

The next morning you step into the bright sun ready to devour the beauty you fully expect to see. The hint of honeysuckle is gone and all you smell is the fragrance of the freshly brewed coffee in your hand.

You glance at the plant and, "Yikes," the blooms that appeared to be on the verge of bursting open just a few hours earlier are now hanging there, limp and drained of all life.

What did I do wrong? What have I done to cause them to die?

Nothing.

This flower graced the world with all it had in one night during the few hours from yesterday afternoon and early this morning and is now gone forever. It reveals itself only to those who are willing to come to it at a time chosen by God.

Sometime after dark the night before the flower quietly opened and announced, "I am here, come see how beautiful I am. Enjoy my wonderful fragrance, but only for a little while."

Few ever see the flower of the night blooming cactus in all its radiant glory or smell the sweet aroma that fills the air because, just before daylight, the bloom wilts and dies.

Many of our lives follow a similar pattern. God prepares us for a task; we perform that task in some private venue with only a few, or maybe no one, realizing that we have done something of great value. By the time others acknowledge us, we have returned to being regular people with no special skills and no obvious beauty.

Most of us live in relative obscurity. We don't attract many accolades from the people we encounter. Only a few people are with us long enough to see that we are pleasing to be around and that we may have something to offer. To those, we are forever beautiful.

Please turn your eyes to those whom God has placed in your path and determine to spend a little more time with them. They may have what you need for this day and this hour.

And for you, continue to bloom where you are and for those who have time for you.

As the Scriptures say, "People are like grass; their beauty is like a flower in the field. The grass withers and the flower fades. But the word of the Lord remains forever. And that word is the Good News that was preached to you." (1 Peter 1:24, 25 NLT)

<u>NOTES</u>

Flawed Perfection

Last Friday, I took several photos of my wife, Carolyn, a couple in full views and one close up. She had been to Coldwater Creek a day earlier and picked up several tops that were on sale. We were about to run some errands when I noticed how nice she looked. I asked her to pose so that I could capture the moment.

As I showed the photos to her, she indicated that she liked the close-up but not the others saying, "They show my flaws."

My response was, "I don't see any flaws. Some of those things you call flaws are what differentiates you from everyone else. It is your own special character."

I described it like when a craftsman purchases material to build something like a boat or a great piece of furniture. Most prefer real wood versus some manufactured substitute, because it has character.

Today, we sat with several friends in a waiting room at Providence hospital while my sister-in-law had surgery to repair damage she sustained to her shoulder in a fall several weeks earlier.

In idle conversation, one of our friends told me that he had always believed he had buck teeth until a dentist told him, "You don't have buck teeth at all, just a serious overbite." The dentist offered to correct it by breaking his jaw in a couple of places and making some adjustments. Jeff said he decided that he liked the way he looked.

I have never noticed anything that detracted from Jeff's appearance, but apparently, he had.

I told him, "God made us all different because we are special. Think of the millions of people in the world, how many of them we cross paths with every day, and how easy it is to recognize someone we know in a crowd of thousands."

I believe that each of us is, in fact, unique.

If you don't think that is special, consider the following definition of unique from *The American Heritage Dictionary*, Second College Edition.

    1. Being the only one of its kind; sole.
    2. Being without equal or equivalent; unparalleled.

    Usage: *Traditional grammarians insist that unique is an "absolute" term—either something is unique, or it isn't—so that it does not allow qualification of degree.*

I would go one step further and use another absolute term to describe you; perfect.

Yeah, we may be able to do a few things to make us appear more attractive to each other or to the mirror, but nothing we do can make us more attractive to God our Father.

Ladies let me clear up a few misconceptions. Most men prefer women with character; women who are honest, trustworthy, and who love us for who we are.

We care a lot less about physical appearance than women believe. We love you just like you are.

You are special because God made you so.

NOTES

He Touched Me

Often while listening to music on the radio, from recorded tapes, CD's, records, or otherwise whenever the urge hits, I will break out singing. More than likely, I am alone when I start my follow-along crooning. *Sweet Home Alabama* by Lynyrd Skynyrd is a personal favorite. Anything by Willie Nelson will certainly spark an outburst.

And then Bill Gaither's *He Touched Me* reminds me of what God has done for me since I committed my life to Jesus. Gaither's words are a testament to what God can and will do to help us through this journey we call life.

As much as I love Jesus Christ, I was touched by someone else long before I ever heard the Gospel.

Who?

Who could compare to the touch of God's gentle hand?

No, I am not being blasphemous when I say someone other than God touched me over a long period of time, nearly thirty-eight years.

How often I wished that we had sat together on a church pew and worshipped God together, at least once. It didn't happen, and I felt short-changed because of it, until. . .

Until the other day. God said to me, "Quit your whining. Don't get hung up on what didn't happen. Let me remind you of the nearly four-decades that you were in his company, and a little of what you received. In fact, his example as a father is what helped you understand My relationship with you. It also helped you through the years you were raising your own children. He helped you understand a father's love and how to share it with your children."

During the time he was on earth, I never heard Daddy sing praises to The Lord. I never sat by his side as he read from the giant Bible emblazoned with the big Masonic symbol on the front cover. It lay unopened on our coffee table most of the time. He never shared wisdom that he credited to learning from God's Word.

The only time I remember being in church with him was at funerals, with one exception. When I was a teenager, I went once to First Baptist Church of Chickasaw, Alabama. On this night, I watched the Reverend Dr. Bob Barker as he performed a ritual that he probably had repeated thousands of times; baptize new converts. On this night, I watched the preacher say a few words, then cover my Daddy's nose, and gently lower him backwards beneath the surface of the water contained in a giant tub located behind the pulpit, and then raise him, "To newness of life."

I didn't understand the significance of this to my Daddy, but Brother Bob referred to it years later as he preached Daddy's funeral.

No, I never sat on a church pew with Daddy, but I would not trade just one time that he and I spent together for a lifetime of being in church with him listening to someone else try to overshadow his wisdom with their ideas.

Daddy seldom set aside formal time for me. He just worked. He worked a lot. He worked two or three jobs. He never wanted his family to suffer the hunger or deprivation that he experienced growing up in the twenties and thirties.

During times that he didn't work for two employers, he used his off-time from that second job to work independently. And I was always invited to join him. He never excused me to go play. Some may ask, "He made you work with him?"

Yes, he did.

Was I upset because I was required to work? No, I enjoyed every minute that we worked together. I loved him and wanted to be with him. He taught me to love what I do and never to think of work as a chore.

He taught me skills that I use regularly thirty-five years after I heard his final words. In his dying moments so long ago, he shared secrets that he had held close to his heart throughout his life.

He taught me carpentry skills as we built things. Together, we built a 24' by 36' garage-workshop. In that garage, he taught me mechanical skills and automotive diagnostics.

There was always someone who needed their car repaired, and Daddy would agree to fix it. We rebuilt engines, transmissions, differentials, and many other components that had failed. After we diagnosed a problem, we would pull the component, tear it down, and prepare it for rebuild. During the next day, Daddy ordered replacement parts for those that were damaged. He expected me to clean and wash all the parts and have them ready to put back together when he got home from his day job.

At night, I watched as he patiently taught me the importance of sequence tightening while installing a crankshaft in a Ford V-8, hydraulic valve lifter adjustment for Chevrolet six's, or how to install the little needle bearings in three speed manual transmissions.

I am sure that he learned many of these skills working with the men in Shubuta, Mississippi who kindly took him under their wing after his daddy, and then his granddaddy, had both passed away before he reached the age of fifteen.

On a rainy night in 1962 before I turned sixteen, he said to me, "Come on."

We drove from our home in Alabama Village all the way across Mobile to the newly opened Springdale Plaza to a jewelry store where Daddy paid a man $350 for a used 1953 Belair Chevrolet convertible. That car had all sorts of problems, and Daddy helped me repair most of them, starting with us replacing the worn-out and leaking top.

It was not a handsome car by any stretch of the imagination, but it carried me back and forth to school, plus on countless other adventures for the next two years.

Daddy told me once, "Son, learn a trade and you will always be able to find work, and you will be able to sleep better at night."

I did that, and I got good at the trade I learned. I had plenty of work, more than my fair share of overtime, and was recognized as an authority in my craft. I did sleep better as I fed my family. It was a satisfying life.

I used to opine about him working too much and never having time to do things that other dads did with their children. Now, I have memories of the man who influenced me way more than I had previously realized.

No, I do not remember sitting beside him in Church, but I sat in his presence countless other times.

He touched me then and continues to do so every day.

Thank You Daddy.

NOTES

A Christmas Lesson

Do you ever feel unworthy? Do you ever wonder why God would Bless you? Do you ever say to yourself, "I wouldn't bless me if I were God?"

Take heart in a truth God revealed to me a few years ago and accept all of God's blessings as a loved child of His.

I learned this valuable lesson from a Christmas morning incident that a friend of the family shared with my dad. Although I received the story second hand, it touched me deeply and opened my heart to a better understanding of my relationship with God.

The family had two sons who were in their late teens when they were blessed with the birth of a little girl. The family loved this child very much and blessed her with as many things as they could afford. Some would say, "They spoiled her."

One Christmas morning, our friend relaxed sipping coffee, delighting himself with the joy he saw in his young daughter's eyes as she ran excitedly from one gift to another. Suddenly, she stopped, pulled her new baby doll close to her heart, and slowly surveyed the floor strewn with torn pieces of brightly colored wrapping paper and many wonderful toys. She then crawled into her daddy's lap, hugged him tightly and asked, "I wonder what Santa Claus would have brought me if I had been good?"

We all had a good laugh from the story, but I later realized that God often treats us like these parents treated that little girl.

I believe that He freely pours out his blessings on us, because He wants to show us the unfettered love from a perfect Father.

I believe that God feels the same way about each one of us and that He thinks of us like what He said about David, "I have found . . . a man after mine own heart." (Acts 13:22 KJV)

That is why I often say, "I have been blessed far beyond what I could have imagined." I follow that up with, "I wonder what God would have done for me if I had only been good?"

NOTES

Mr. Wonderful

I often refer to myself as "Mr. Wonderful." Not because I think I am such a much, but because of a perceptive observation by one of my wife's, best friends.

Jennie didn't watch me and say, "Wow, Wayne is such a wonderful person, nearly perfect. I believe that we should call him, 'Mr. Wonderful.'" No, if she had seen all my actions, those words would never have come out of her mouth.

Carolyn, my wife, and Jennie's friendship began more than two decades ago when they ministered together in a Christian Women's organization. As they reached out to help other women, they often shared their own concerns with each other, and soon became each other's strongest encouragers. I am sure that Carolyn shared with Jennie some of those times when I fell short of God's expectations for me. It was not to be critical, but to seek confidential agreement in prayer for my best interests.

I believe Jennie listened to Carolyn talk about our life and noted that Carolyn said very little that portrayed me in a negative light. I know that Carolyn is so ingrained in my life that she sees clearly most every fault and shortcoming I have. Make no mistake; she is not shy when she wants to make me aware of changes I need to make to improve me.

Jennie did not hear a lot of nitpicking about my shortcomings. Instead, she heard mostly positive characteristics accredited to me. She naturally thought more of me. I am pretty sure Carolyn did not brag about how wonderful and perfect I am. She likely spoke of our love for each other and the children of our union. She probably pointed out that we always work together to maintain the integrity of our family relationship. In so doing, Carolyn chose to create life in me with her words rather than to sacrifice me on an altar of imperfection.

"Death and Life are in the power of the tongue." (Proverbs 18:21 KJV) This verse makes it clear that we hold unique powers to use our conversation to either create life or to destroy it.

The New Living Translation says it a little more clearly: "Those who love to talk will experience the consequences, for the tongue can kill or nourish life." (Proverbs 18:21 NLT)

I appreciate the fact that Carolyn chooses to see the things I do that are right and spends little time focusing on my faults. In so doing, she encourages me to work especially hard to maintain that level of faith she has in me.

I do not take criticism well, especially mean-spirited words that are spoken to destroy, but I do respond, much like the family pet, to encouraging words that assure me I am loved. If I had a long bushy tail, it would be wagging wildly in response to Carolyn's loving and encouraging words.

Thanks, Jennie, for your encouraging nickname.

NOTES

Overcoming Failure

Failure is part of our lives. Often, we may ask ourselves, what if I had only done this or that another way? Could those different actions change the consequences of the mistakes? Consider the following two events where I could have made better decisions.

My initial thought—The way to grow is to be allowed to fail. However, as a parent, when it comes to our children, we do not ever want to fail. Consider a young man teaching his daughter to ride a bicycle.

The first incident happened on Christmas day in 1970. Santa Claus had brought my six-year-old daughter, Tammi, a brand new 20" bicycle, complete with training wheels that would help her learn to ride. Now it is time to plan the event. What do I do?

I adjust the training wheels so that they will keep her from turning over if she loses her balance. I adjust the seat where Tammi's feet rest comfortably on the pedals. I adjust the handlebar so that she can safely steer while she sits on the seat. She had been riding a tricycle, so she understood the concept of pedaling.

I rolled her out near the street, turned her and the bicycle around so that she faced the house. I told her,

"When I let go, start pedaling and steer straight down the sidewalk toward the house." With everything in order, I give her a slight shove and tell her to go. Perfect. She is pedaling directly toward her goal. I have done my job.

At the precise time that I calculated in my head that would allow her ample time to stop, I yell out, "Step on the brakes!"

She screams back, "Brakes! What's that?" Oh no, maybe I didn't do my job so well.

I ran after her and caught her just after she hit the house. Thankfully, neither her nor the bicycle are damaged. Thank you, God, for protecting her when her daddy didn't.

Note to self: *Don't overlook key details in your life, your family, or your job.* It can have serious negative consequences. Do your best to consider all actions required for a successful outcome.

NOTES

Overcoming Failure Again

The second incident is perhaps the greatest failure in my life.

Russell, the biggest kid in the ninth grade at K. J. Clark Junior High School, and Charles, one of the smallest kids had gotten in a scrap during our physical education class. When they didn't get it settled during class, Russell promised to take care of it at the end of the school day.

Enter this author, aka the fixer. Long story short, I told Russell, "If you want to fight Charles, you will have to whip me first." The dumbest thing that I have ever said in my life, thus my greatest mistake. Those words have never come out of my mouth again.

Russell responded, "That's okay with me."

His first swing blackened my left eye, the second swing blackened my right eye, the third broke my nose. I don't know how many more swings were involved. By this time, I was in a semi-conscious stupor and did not want to stop. Several kids stepped in to pull me free from the beating that I was enduring. I finally turned and walked toward home, lonely and dejected.

When I came back to school the next day, both Russell and I were called to the principal's office.

The readers should be happy to know the principal made Russell apologize to me. His apology really didn't sound sincere to me, but by then I was biased against Russell.

It would be horrible, if the story ended there.

This incident changed my life goal. Until this happened, I was sending for material on law schools and seriously considered going into the legal profession. I considered this to be my first case, and I lost miserably. I considered it unhealthy to base my life goals on my failed argumentative skills from this incident. The only thing worse is my skill as a fighter.

I have learned since this incident, to work together for common goals. I have spent the rest of my life working with others to accomplish something, never wanting to fight physically or in arguments. That is why my wife, Carolyn, and I get along. We do not fight. We don't always agree, but we never fight.

I am thankful for one good result from this incident. I never had another fight. In school, some classmates may have believed if I would fight the biggest kid in school, they couldn't bully me, and they were not sure if they could whip me or not.

As it turned out, my greatest failure led to my greatest success. It would be years later, when Dinty Walston, the loveable SOB from another story, and the manager I reported to on a major project, asked in a meeting, "Wayne, what is your philosophy in a barroom brawl?"

I quickly responded, "Drop to the floor and crawl to the door."

He just smiled and said, "I like that."

Thank You, Father, for teaching me at such a young age how to settle disagreements. Thank you also for my failures that have resulted in me having the wonderful life that I am now living.

NOTES

Renewal

This is an update to the previous story in this book, *Overcoming Failure Again*. In it I described how my desire to solve all problems can be my undoing.

At our 50th high school reunion a classmate, Steve Maples, who was familiar with my earlier story, and who knew all participants in that great debate, had a little fun at my expense.

In my early days I had a desire to become a lawyer when I grew up. I suspect interest died after unsuccessfully arguing my first case. The prize for losing was a good ole fashion butt-whipping in front of much of the student body.

Anyway, Steve, who went on to become a criminal defense attorney, had a lot of fun razzing me about who may or may not be at the class reunion, and even though it had been more than fifty years since I lost that fight, Russell could likely do it again if he showed up. Steve finally acknowledged that he had talked with Russell and I didn't have to worry. Russell was not coming. Thank God I didn't have to re-address that debate.

If only Steve had taken the earlier case, maybe there would have been a better outcome for me. I can't say what would have happened to Steve if he lost the original argument. Maybe I would have been writing my earlier story about him?

Now that we have had a little fun with the story, I can report a perfect outcome.

We were having some bathroom remodeling done on our house and the contractor had pretty-well tried our patience. He promised to complete the work in five days, but after dealing with several of his well-meaning, but incompetent sub-contractors, the job was in its third month.

One small task remaining was to replace a linen closet door. It was obvious this sub-contractor didn't have the expertise to replace the door without botching it. I had seen several of his suggested options. After complaining to my primary contractor, I was assured they would get a cabinet maker to install a new door.

The next day I received a telephone call. The voice on the other end of the line said, "Mr. Brady, my name is Chuck and I need to come out and take measurements to replace a cabinet door."

I said ok, and we settled on a day and time. Afterwards, the voice asked me, "Did you grow up in Prichard?"

"Yes," I said.

"Did you live in Alabama Village?"

"Yes."

"Did you go to Clark school?"

"Yes."

"I think I know you."

I responded, "I don't remember anyone named Chuck from school."

He said, "I was called Charles back then. Charles Hatchett."

My response was quick and clear, "Oh yeah, I remember you. I took an a** whipping for you."

He said, "I very well remember that. You are not going to punch me in the nose when I come over, are you?"

"No, I'm not. We were good friends, and I am looking forward to seeing you."

To make this story a little shorter, we had a wonderful time reminiscing about our youthful days, and we have renewed a far too-long estranged friendship. I have since met Charles' beautiful wife Rose and had the pleasure of their company at our high school reunion.

When I think about the frustrating experience dealing with a poor performing remodeler, I am reminded that without some of the issues we had, I may have lived the rest of my life without the fellowship of an old friend.

I love it when God works all things together for my good. (Romans 8:28 paraphrase)

NOTES

Emotions-Love-Assurance

The quiet solitude; silence, then the soft gentle touch of the cool morning air stimulating my senses.

My emotions were nothing like twelve hours earlier. More than a hundred thousand fans shouting for our team or singing Lynyrd Skynyrd's *Sweet Home Alabama*, Garth Brooks' *I got friends in low places*, and finally Alabama's *Dixieland Delight*.

The dichotomy of an uproarious, "Roll Tide Roll," permeating the air such a short time ago, and now only the occasional soft sound of "Old Glory" moving gently on the giant crane a hundred and fifty feet above my head.

The smooth folding sound of fabric reminded me of my grandmother who, like a fisherman spreading his net, gently layered my bed with sheets and blankets as she tucked me in for a relaxing night in my safe place.

Emotions, last night the highest, and now the sweetest. God is so good to me.

I am reminded of the eternal love from our heavenly Father by the earthly example of my father for his son, and my grandmother's unabated affection for her child's child. All are unmeasurable, infinite, and without boundaries.

Those are two of the most unselfish assurances that every child should receive. They are perfect examples of God's Love for us.

I pray that you have received similar assurances from some of the people in your life. If you have not, feel free to contact me, and I will help you.

NOTES

God is in Control

When Carolyn and I married we were pretty much in agreement on life in general. We understood there may be conflict over time, but we figured we would work it out. I had lived twenty-one years, and we never had problems in my family that we could not work out, or that would destroy our family unit.

For the most part, Carolyn and I did not argue. I only remember a couple of times, and those didn't consume our lives. We never went to bed thinking, *this is hard, maybe we have made a bad decision, or maybe we should end this thing.*

In fact, our son commented one time, "It is hard for me to find a lady that will give me the sort of life y'all have. I don't ever remember y'all arguing, certainly not in front of us."

We did have a rule that we did not argue in front of the children. Neither did we take sides in a disagreement one of us may have had with one of our children. Our unwritten, but understood rule was to support the other when we were with the children. When we were alone, we often talked about a choice that one made, that may not have been the best. If we determined we could have done better, we admitted it, and then together we went back to the children and reversed our decision. We always wanted them to know we were going to agree on all conclusions concerning them. We knew that we could not be at odds with each other, if we and our family were to survive.

All of that said, we agreed on two rules before we married in the event we ever had a son, and then we set out to get on with life.

Rule Number One—Our son would never play football.

Carolyn explained that her brother-in-law played in high school and had sustained permanent back damage. Some of the high school coaches didn't take him seriously when he said he was hurt, and continued to play him after hearing his complaints, even called him names like sissy and chicken to shame him back onto the field.

I didn't play football, and I didn't care if our son played. I didn't like physical education, didn't like participating in team sports, and I rarely dressed out for our normal PE classes and did not take it my senior year. I didn't like the coaches. They were overbearing and always trying to intimidate us. I was not easily intimidated.

Rule Number Two—Our son would never own a BB gun.

Carolyn was concerned about who or what our son may shoot. Carolyn had an older cousin who had shot her on several occasions.

My daddy bought a BB gun for my brother when we were young. Then daddy left us alone outside. My brother, three years older than me, decided it would be fun to shoot at a moving target. So, he challenged me, his five-year-old brother, to be his target. He said he would give me to the count of three to get far enough away before he would start shooting.

He was pretty accurate and was able to plant several welts on my bare back, when the shooting was done.

It would be nine years before we addressed either of these two rules again. We were too busy making a living, raising our children, and dealing with more pressing problems.

It was bound to happen. Our son, Gary, was five years-old when he was exposed to football. There were children in our neighborhood who played youth sports, one played football. Gary noticed the pads that he wore as he left his house to go to practice.

Occasionally, we watched football games on TV with family and friends. Gary didn't fully understand the concept, but he often mimicked what he saw on TV. He would stand and watch the action on screen and then run, fall, and roll doing his best to imitate actions he had just witnessed.

We mentioned Gary's behavior to a friend and he just laughed it off. The next time he came over, he had a gift for Gary. He said it was one that his boys had when they were Gary's size. Gary beamed when Marvin handed him his gift. In a moment, Gary had ripped his shirt off and pulled this pint-sized replica of LSU's away jersey over his head.

Carolyn and I found some imitation shoulder pads at Sears and Roebuck. Gary was thrilled to pull on these innocent reproductions for a grown-up game, and would not take them off, not even for bed. There were many nights that he fell asleep wearing them.

When it came time to sign up for youth football, Gary asked if he could play. Initially, Carolyn and I said, "No."

We could no longer ignore the issue that we didn't want to address at this stage of our life. Together we decided, if Gary wanted to play, we would turn it over to our Father in Heaven.

We prayed, "Father, we do not want Gary to play this sport that could be really dangerous. However, because he wants to play on his own, we will allow Gary to play if You will protect him. He is our son, You gave him to us, and we ask You to watch over him as he pursues his dreams. Please protect him."

That year, we signed him up for youth football. He turned six-years-old after practice started. He didn't play a lot, only a few plays per game, but the next year, we had moved and signed him up at another park.

He understood more about what they were doing and what the goals of the game were. The coaches recognized his intense desire to play. He always listened and learned fast. The coaches used him in several key positions, on both offense and defense. He played nearly a hundred percent of every game.

We prayed for him on every play.

He loved it so much that he continued to play all the way through his growing up years, through high school, and then earned a scholarship to play football in college. He played two years at Lindenwood College in Saint Charles, Missouri, before he decided his playing days were over.

Sometimes agreements can be amended or changed. We did eventually bend on the no BB gun allowed rule. I taught Gary to respect the gun, never to point it at anyone or anything that he didn't want to shoot. I have that BB gun at our house right now.

We allowed our children to make most of their own decisions in life, gave those decisions to God, and we are thankful for how well each has turned out.

Thank You, Father, for the family you placed in my care, please forgive me where I failed, and things could have gone really bad. Thank you for redeeming my mistakes. I Love You, and I love my wife, my children, and grandchildren.

NOTES

The Goodness of God

The couple sat talking quietly about the future knowing the waitress would return soon with their hamburgers and milk shakes. He dropped a couple of quarters into the miniature jukebox mounted next to their table and stared off in the distance, half listening to the music playing softly in the background. It reminded him of a time long ago, the only difference being the music would have been a lot louder then.

She reached across the table and took his hand and said softly, "You know I love you."

"Yes," he replied redirecting his gaze into her beautiful brown eyes.

The waitress interrupted their exchange as she placed a plate in front of each of them. She added two frosted glasses that were filled to the rim. One nearly overflowing with a savory white dessert, and the other with rich chocolate, both topped off with a creamy mound of whipped cream resembling the snowcapped Smokey Mountains at Christmas. "May I bring you anything else?"

"No, this is fine," she said as she put the straw in her mouth and took a big slurp of the vanilla shake. "That is good."

He poured a little mustard on the bottom half of his hamburger bun and spread it around with his knife. He stopped and took a sip of his chocolate shake and then looked up at her. "These are good shakes."

"Do you think they are better than Tom's?"

He squeezed the ketchup over the mustard in a spiral motion until the bun was nearly covered. He then placed the pickles, onions, and meat over the red and yellow goo. He added the tomato and lettuce, and then topped it off with the sesame seed bun. "I don't know," he replied. He enjoyed the Big Time Diner's food. However, the best thing was that it reminded him of days gone by.

Tom's was one of those good memories. Tom's Dairy Freeze was a favorite hangout of teenagers in the fifties and sixties. He had worked there during his senior year of high school.

In a moment, he was transported back there as if in a time machine, to the night they met. The Vietnam War was raging heavily, and he had recently returned home from his U. S. Army Reserve basic military training and was visiting with Tom. He had free run of the place, although he had not worked there in years. He was about to prepare a chocolate shake for himself when she walked to the window. He had known her from school but had not seen her in more than five years. He told Tom, "I will wait on this customer."

"I haven't seen you in a long time. You do look really nice. What'll you have?" He asked looking her up and down. *She is beautiful,* he thought.

"Two single cones of black walnut and two of soft vanilla," she said smiling broadly. "I haven't been around in a long time."

"I'll be right back."

He returned in a few moments with the two cones of Tom's special recipe black walnut for her and her sister. The spiral topped cones of soft vanilla were for the two small girls seated in the back seat of her father's car. "Here you go. That'll be twenty-five cents."

She fumbled around in her purse, pulled out a case quarter, handed it to him, and said, "I didn't know you worked here."

He stood holding the quarter in his hand and replied, "I don't. I was just getting me something to eat when I saw you walk up. I had to wait on you. Are you available?"

"I'm not married if that's what you mean," she answered maintaining her beautiful smile.

"Are you looking for a husband?" He asked.

"No. Are you looking for a wife?"

"No. Will you go to the fair with me this weekend?"

"Sure."

It was that easy. Neither was looking for a permanent relationship. Maybe that is why all their friends were surprised when they married in less than four months.

"What would you like for Christmas?" she asked, breaking the silence, and causing him to return instantly to the present.

"I haven't thought about it." Since they had been together, he had experienced a lifetime of joy and happiness.

They had married two days before Christmas after a whirlwind romance that was more exciting than anything he had ever witnessed in the movies. They planned to marry a day earlier, on Friday night after work, but the local justice of the peace was sick and unavailable. They were forced to postpone their plans until Saturday morning, and hope they could locate another judicial officer who could unite them in holy wedlock.

After an early morning telephone call, they made the two-hour drive to Grove Hill, the closest county government agency open on Saturday. They walked briskly into the licensing area holding hands and smiling.

One of the ladies looked up and said, "We know what you are in here for. Come over here, I will take care of you."

After a few minutes of filling out the obligatory paperwork, he paid for the marriage license and asked, "Is there anyone around who can marry us?"

"The judge is in and he will be happy to do it."

The honeymoon included lunch at Deavers Restaurant in Grove Hill, a three-hour drive to Pensacola, a stop at K-Mart for some food, and a quiet dinner alone in their rented furnished house.

The following morning, they rose early, and traveled to Mobile to prepare Christmas for the two beautiful children who were staying with her parents. This was their first of many happy Christmases together.

That day he gained a completely new family who accepted him right from the start. In addition to Carolyn, Tammi, and Terri, there was Mom, Granddaddy, and Debra. They all gave him love and treated him with the utmost respect. He and Ray (Granddaddy) became hunting and fishing buddies and best friends, and they grew closer and closer over the next thirty years. Debra was dating Frank while they attended Vigor High School and would marry him soon after graduation.

Three years later, Christmas became more special because in addition to having a wonderful wife, he had petitioned for and been granted the right and privilege to become the girls Daddy. The judge had commented that he could see the joy and pleasure on his face, and that he would surely be acting in the girls' best interests to grant them to him, as his legally adopted heirs.

In another year, Christmas became even more special after the birth of a son who served to add another dimension to their family.

There have been more than fifty Christmases since that first meeting at Tom's, and each one has been more precious than the previous, with the exception that Mom and Granddaddy are no longer with them.

The Perfect Dad

The 23rd Psalm is a blueprint for who a father should be.

Example: My earthly Dad (and this could be written about millions of others, not just mine) presented the perfect example of the shepherd father, and he did it without going to church very often. Although, I believe we should take our family to meet with other Christians in corporate worship to learn about God and who He is, it is not an absolute requirement for being a good father.

I did not worship my dad, but I do remember him teaching me with gentle, loving kindness his entire life.

I know many dads fulfill their responsibilities to their families, but I am also aware that some fall short. We all do at times.

Father, I pray that you minister to the daddy's right here in America, that you encourage them to be good fathers, and that you instill wisdom in each of them, In Jesus' Name.

The table that follows offers a comparison.

This is how Daddy fulfilled the 23rd Psalm

Daddy, You Fulfilled		Psalms 23:1-6 KJV
You were my protector, I never wanted for anything that I needed.	1	*The Lord is my shepherd; I shall not want.*
Thank you for a stable peaceful home for me to rest and renew my mind and body.	2	*He maketh me to lie down in green pastures: he leadeth me beside the still waters.*
You continuously encouraged me and always taught me the right way to live.	3	*He restoreth my soul: he leadeth me in the paths of righteousness for his name's sake.*
Even when I was in scary places, I was not afraid. Your strength comforted me. I knew I was safe beside you.	4	*Yea, though I walk through the valley of the shadow of death, I will fear no evil: for thou art with me; thy rod and thy staff they comfort me.*
You provided food for our family and you protected us from all enemies. How often I ran to your open loving arms. I am so blessed.	5	*Thou preparest a table before me in the presence of mine enemies: thou anointest my head with oil; my cup runneth over.*
Your loving kindness fulfilled me your entire life. I lived in your house, and you will be a part of me forever.	6	*Surely goodness and mercy shall follow me all the days of my life: and I will dwell in the house of the Lord for ever.*

Thank You Daddy, for being a wonderful example for me. You made it easy for me to transfer our relationship characteristics to a relationship with God our Father. It also became a pattern for me when I was raising our children. I could not have made it without you.

Thank You, Pastor Jim Kinder, for inspiring me to write this.

NOTES

My Life is Like a Hallmark Movie

Have you ever watched a Hallmark movie? In many, if not most, the plot centers on a protagonist who has lost touch with someone he should cherish and want to be with. Most of the time the separation is the choice of the protagonist, but sometimes the decision is by others.

Watching these movies, I have been amazed when a person would get so disenchanted or frustrated about something that he would cut off all communication with someone that he should otherwise be bound to forever, either by blood or relationship.

I shouldn't be surprised with these plots because they only reflect real life situations. I personally know too many families with estranged members; sons, daughters, parents, siblings, other relatives, or past friends. Until recently, I didn't fully comprehend how people could live a lifetime of separation. No, not until it happened to me.

I have several people who I was very close to who have decided that I am not worth their time or trouble. I don't live in a fantasy land and I understand that my words and actions may have set in motion their decision. My being sorry or my apologies are not enough to restore our fellowship. Maybe one day. Until then I am forced to carry on without their smile, without their touch, without their fellowship; without them.

It's bad enough that they have stopped communication with me, but I really don't understand why they have severed ties with Carolyn, my wife.

Since I have lived my life as "Mr. Fix-it," I am at a loss for how to resolve the problems when all communication is cut-off. I am told that in time some may review their decision and consider allowing me back in their life.

Now, when I see other families with estranged members, I understand their pain, and I know better how to pray.

I do not write this to gain sympathy for my plight, but to help others who may be struggling because they don't get to be with someone they treasure. Please know that God has not forgotten you. He will send others to fill the void. No, it may not be the same as what you lost but it is God telling you that you are loved, and that He will take care of you. Be thankful for every person God brings through your life. They could be angels God has sent to encourage you.

Father, I pray that you fix hearts. Show me what I can do. Restore the joy of renewed fellowship in our life with family and friends. I also ask you to minister to all who read these words. I ask for all of this in Jesus' name.

Despised and Rejected

None of what follows is written as if I am an expert on the subject I am writing about. It is just one south Alabama boy's interpretation of life as I understand it. Even if you are not a Christian, I believe that you will benefit from what I advocate at the end.

Sometimes, I wake up with my mind in gear and running at full speed. Often, I am thinking about what I need to do, most likely something I have neglected. Other times I may have a new idea on how to tackle an old problem. And then occasionally, I wake up with a revelation that clearly defines something that I did not understand to this point. Sunday, January 4, 2015 was a morning for the latter.

Please forgive me, but I believe that revelation of something I never knew before comes from someone more intelligent than me, and someone who knew I needed it, someone who loves me unconditionally. That someone is God, the Creator of this wonderful world we live in.

During this early hour, God opened my eyes, and gave me a glimpse at what Jesus endured during His brief time on earth. Not only was He rejected among men, He was also DESPISED by the very people He lived and ultimately died for.

I believe the reason God revealed this is to help me better empathize with other people who have been ostracized from their family or circle of friends.

Many families are broken apart—some members rejected and despised—for countless reasons or misunderstandings. Mine is not to judge why they are where they are, but to be in prayerful sympathy for them, and to continue to offer support and forgiveness. It is God's job to bring the conviction that will cause hearts to change.

The scripture predicted that Jesus would not be received by all. "He is despised and rejected of men; a man of sorrows, and acquainted with grief: and we hid as it were our faces from him; he was despised, and we esteemed him not." (Isaiah 53:3 KJV)

I learned about rejection in the mid-seventies when we attended Bayview Heights Baptist Church in Mobile, Alabama. No, it was not my first experience with rejection; it was just the first time I had it diagnosed and defined to me. Pastor Sam Phillips preached about it, and both he and his wife, Gloria, taught about it. They helped me understand it is natural for all of us to feel rejected from time to time.

I learned that when people do not like me and openly reject me, it affects me, but it only becomes a real problem when I turn inward and dwell on it. It's not a big deal if someone I encounter ignores me or does not want a friendship with me. Frankly, there are some people we like from the moment we meet, and others we never seem to have a connection with. It is a natural way that we choose friends and develop long-term relationships.

My wife, Carolyn, is the first person I recognized that truly accepted me for who I am. Her belief in me instead of focusing on the things in me that may have turned others away caused me to begin understanding myself. Looking back, I realize many others loved and accepted me, and I have since worked to cultivate those relationships.

Back to rejection. I have received consistent and unwarranted rejection from a few people throughout my life. Not just from some who have no reason to develop a connection with me, but also from some who should desire to be a part of my life.

It is hard for me to believe that I have been rejected by so many, but not nearly as tough as when I realized that I am despised by a few. What have I done to be so hated? I freely admit that I may have done some pretty bad things, but nothing—I believe—that should be unforgivable.

It is bad enough when people reject us as a result of our own actions, but it is something quite different when they discard us outright with no apparent reason. And, when they start believing something that is not true to maintain their position, it becomes an immovable obstacle to healing our relationships.

Despicable me! Don't feel sorry for me. Love me. God will touch the hearts of all, and many will change their position toward me; others may not.

How would I understand God without realizing that Jesus came to offer hope to His people, the Jewish nation? After many rejected and despised Him, our Father turned to us, an undeserving world, and adopted us into His family.

Our Father simply said to all who would hear and believe that Jesus Christ is His Son, sent from heaven, to save us from ourselves, "To them gave He the power to become the sons of God." (John 1:12 KJV)

We have been adopted into His heavenly family and have been lifted to the status of being a brother to Jesus.

Jesus said, "O Jerusalem, Jerusalem, which killest the prophets, and stonest them that are sent unto thee; how often would I have gathered thy children together, as a hen doth gather her brood under her wings, and ye would not!" (Luke 13:34 KJV)

To those who may have people in your life that you look down on with contempt, even to the point that you loathe them, or think of them as worthless, please consider the harm you are doing to yourself, and ask our Father to instill forgiveness in you. It will free you to better understand our Father.

If you are on the receiving end of rejection or hatred, forgive them and pray for them. Ask our Father to remind them of your love for them. You don't have to be perfect, only accessible.

I lift up all who read these words, and I pray for healed relationships in your life in Jesus' name.

Believe

This is not a political post, but my thoughts about God and Christianity. I accepted Jesus a long time ago, and I am of the mind that each of us should make that decision based on our own examinations of the various theories of God's existence.

I have never been afraid for others to argue a case against my beliefs, but atheists don't seem to share that opinion. It is as if they are afraid if someone hears The Word, he will be converted to Christianity. They must believe there is something to reading or hearing God's Word. They certainly know there is no power in their cold dead words.

I imagine it takes more faith to believe there is no God than to trust in Him, after hearing arguments atheists make in support of science.

There is general agreement in the scientific community that there are too many unknowns for anyone to state definitively how earth, life on it, or when and how the universe came to be. They don't even agree on if the universe began with one event, or if there was something before that.

Folks who like to tout science over theology fail to understand that we as Christians don't have a problem if God decided to start the universe with a big bang that created our solar system with the earth, moon, sun, and cycles for all living things. It makes sense to me that a "Master Intelligent Being" that we know simply as God or Father, designed it all.

We only have to watch one human "Master" of anything working meticulously to develop his creation, to understand that we are one complex piece of a "Great Creative Design."

Science is not our issue. Uncertainty in the scientific community is a problem for scientists, and for everyone else.

Cosmologists like to point to the big bang theory which concludes that after a cataclysmic explosion, everything as we know it, was just here. All the pieces and parts from the explosion randomly settled into a perfect combination that formed the universe, separated the earth off into an exact blend of the elements to support life, started plants growing, and then formed the animal kingdom. Of course, man is the highest form of intelligence that we know about, complete with a brain to observe the world around him, inquisitive enough to study scientific details of all things, and with great reasoning to judge all he sees.

Such an explosion, defying all laws of physics, to create everything as we know it would be a miracle. And, if there has ever been just one miracle, there could have been others; then all of science is in doubt.

The next two paragraphs of notes and quotes are from the September 2013 on-line issue of Discover magazine. Steve Nadis, the writer of the article dated Thursday, October 10, 2013, states, "Cosmologist Alexander Vilenkin believes the big bang was a series of big bangs that created an endless number of bubble universes".

Vilenkin said, "We have very good evidence that there was a Big Bang."

"Vilenkin says . . . The universe had a distinct beginning - though he can't pinpoint the time. . . he's found that before our universe there was nothing, nothing at all, not even time itself."

Personally, I think an explosion of nothing in nothing would be to quote William Shakespeare, "Much Ado About Nothing."

Vilenkin's assertion that there was no time before the big bang confirms a future God has planned for us when time again, will be no more.

Then there are the atheists who like to call themselves free thinkers, who believe anything scientists say.

Free thinkers' definition 1: A person who forms his or her own opinions about important subjects (such as religion and politics), instead of accepting what other people say.

Duh, that's what we all do. I expect most atheists listen to others and very much form their opinions based on what other unbelievers say. Makes them pretty much like those of us who form our opinions based on the testimony of other believers.

Free thinkers' definition 2: One who forms opinions on the basis of reason independently of authority; especially one who doubts or denies religious dogma.

I would say all of us are free thinkers in that sense. A decision on whether to believe or not should be based on our own reasoning, looking at as much information as possible versus what someone else says. The difference in believers is that God will speak to the individual, in this case me, and make Himself real to me or you.

By definition, unbelievers cannot see what may be right there in front of them. They should not let obstinacy keep them from God's promised blessing.

I contend atheists are not free to think what they want at all. They must follow the principles espoused before them, or they are wrong. One would think they would be open to allow everyone to think freely, but that is not true at all.

They cannot remain in their groups if they begin to doubt their conclusion that there is no God, and any re-examination that may result in a belief that there is a God blows their hypocritical minds.

If everyone who calls himself a free thinker comes to the same conclusion, I suggest they are not free thinkers at all but worshippers at a different assemblage.

Most of what I see from atheists is, they are intolerant, and they like to call Christians hurtful names in an apparent effort to try and prove a point.

Jesus was perfectly clear when He asserted that those who believe in Him, must come to Him as a child, with complete faith and trust in Him.

Jesus said, "Verily I say unto you, Except ye be converted, and become as little children, ye shall not enter into the kingdom of heaven." (Matthew 18:3 KJV)

I have weighed the arguments and my beliefs are settled. I came through my journey of discovery as an adult and I won't entertain unbelief. It is not that I am not free to question. It's just that I am settled in the Truth.

You are free to believe as you want.

Dear friends, scientists merely present limited evidence, not actual proof as some claim, to argue their theory. They presume we will accept their testimony on faith. Evidence is what lawyers argue over to convince a jury to vote their way. Is this a court of scientific opinion?

Then this jurist votes in favor of a one true God. Case closed.

NOTES

A Lifetime of Work

I told a friend one day that I enjoyed my job, and he quickly retorted, "I have never liked even one day at work in my whole life." We were both 65 at the time, and he couldn't understand why I would continue to get up early and spend the day going to a job.

I will admit that I have not enjoyed every job that I have had. I certainly have not enjoyed every task that was assigned to me, but I am thankful for all.

I often tell people my daddy taught me how to work, not how to vacation. He told me once, "Learn a trade and you will always be able to find work, and when you get a steady job, you will be able to sleep nights."

How did he come up with such a policy?

Daddy's family was normal for the small community where he lived. His daddy, my granddaddy, was an engineer on a logging train, a hard-working man who loved to hunt and fish. One night after work, already showing flu-like symptoms, he chose to go out in the cold rain to get some meat for the family table. It was a successful trip, but it turned out to be very costly for him and the family, when he developed a severe case of pneumonia and died a few days later.

My daddy was only nine-years old, and he had younger siblings to mentor. The great depression was in its early stages. Money was tight, but his granddaddy, the local blacksmith, helped as much as he could. He taught his young grandson how to shoe horses, how to bond two pieces of metal together, how to repair broken wagon wheels, and other tasks. He paid him for his work around the forge. This helped feed the family for the next six years, but then his grandfather passed away.

The family was suddenly even poorer than before. My daddy, at the age of 15, took on the role of primary bread winner, quit school and began a lifetime of work, to make sure there would always be food on his family's table. He never complained and always expressed his gratitude to the men of Shubuta, Mississippi who taught him mechanical skills, and who provided paying work for him.

Just like his granddaddy, daddy and his younger brother hunted nights, often coming in late with fresh meat. When they did, my grandmother would get out of bed, prepare the first family meal of the day, and the family would gather around the candle-lit table, and be thankful for the fresh biscuits and rabbit smothered in gravy.

My daddy always worked, and I got to know him working beside him. We never went on a vacation to a tourist destination; we never got to put a bumper sticker on our car that read, "See Rock City," like some of my friends. If the family went anywhere, it was to visit relatives, and I loved it. I still maintain close relationships with many of the cousins I got to know during those trips.

My Daddy, never said, "I love you," but I watched him be patient and kind to everyone he met, and I knew with every action that he made toward me, he loved me as much as any father ever loved a son. He taught me to work hard, treat others fairly, be honest, and I trusted him with my life. He taught me how to fix things, and he loved my mother.

I followed his advice about keeping a steady job for a long time, but there came a day when I realized that I was different. It was after hearing that great philosopher, Evel Knievel, in an interview (right before one of his infamous jumps), respond to a question about how he could continue to perform such dangerous stunts. Knievel said, I would rather die trying to do something I want to do, than to live and never try anything (paraphrase).

All I wanted to do was change jobs, so I quit a very good civil service job, and started a lifetime of trusting God to provide for me and my family. I have never regretted it.

There have been some lean times when I found myself without a job, but I have never collected unemployment insurance or welfare, and my family has never gone hungry.

All this rambling to say that I am not troubled by working. In fact, I enjoy it. I work part time now and I consider myself fortunate to work for people who are flexible enough to allow me to continue in a limited role. If I die without ever being fully retired, I have lived a satisfying life of service to others, both paid and voluntary.

Thank You Daddy, for instilling your work ethic in me.

NOTES

ENCOURAGEMENT FOR THE AGES

Stories to remind us it is never too early and never too late to receive a new vision from God. Whatever your age, feel free to set new goals and to turn in a different direction. God will go with you.

Part One—Thirties & Forties

How old is too old? 30? 60? 100? I don't know. When I get there, I will tell you. Even though I move slower, feel pain more quickly, and go to the doctor more often, I believe that I have not reached the full potential God intends for me. I proclaim that I am still in the early stages of my life even though I am three years past the age my grandmother believed we are allotted.

Miss Hattie, MawVall to us grandchildren, told me, "Anyone older than seventy is living on borrowed time." I suspect she read, "The days of our years are threescore years and ten;" (Psalm 90:10 KJV). The interesting part of her life is that she died at the age of seventy, just as she believed.

Is age 30 too old?

Several years ago, I responded to a friend who was feeling old because she had just turned thirty, "Happy Birthday My Friend, enjoy every minute of this day as if it is your last, but understand you are likely to live two more of your lifetimes. It may be the largest number of years for you, but likely it's less than a third of the years that you will someday reach. That in mind, always be ready to embark on any path you think you may want to try. There is more than enough time to reach your destination and plenty of time to heal all ills. You have time to change careers three or four times."

No, it's not 30. God will bless the decade of your thirties and fill them with wonderful opportunities for growth. Remember, Jesus started His ministry at the very young age of thirty and made an eternal impact for mankind by the time He was thirty-three years old.

What about age 40? On the same day that I wrote the preceding, another person read it and asked, "Do you have a word for me, a forty-year-old?"

I responded, "I am not sure if you are asking tongue-in-cheek, but I am going to assume you really want to know. First, for you babies who are in your forties, you likely have one and a third more lifetimes (or more) to live. Fifty plus years are more than enough to do anything you may want with your life, or to accomplish any goal that you may have previously set aside.

Second, if you have children, they are likely about to be grown, and you will have to decide what you want to do with the rest of your life. You may even have grandchildren that you are spoiling.

Third, you have a better understanding of what is important in life. In my own life, I went back to school at age 44 after my boss suggested that I take some classes to improve my job skills. I took a few classes and discovered I loved learning and eventually fell in love with writing. It took a few years, but I graduated magna-cum-laude from The

University of Alabama in 1998 at the age of 52. If you are interested, I can tell you of some programs that make learning enjoyable, and relatively easy to take classes and earn a degree while working full time."

To all ages, please accept my words as encouragement. Realize how young you are, and step back into the future. As in the well-known cliché, "Today is the first day of the rest of your life." If you get knocked down, get up. Sometimes it may take a few days or longer to get over life's challenges, but you can do it.

God Bless You!

NOTES

Part Two—Fifties

I realize that we are often guilty of believing that our present age, whatever age that may be, is the ending stage of our life. However, with a little encouragement, and as long as there is breath in our bodies, God still has something for us to accomplish.

Our problem? We tend to believe that what God wants us to accomplish is something big in the spiritual world. We would like to be a Peter or Paul, or some great evangelist, or pen the words to a fresh new revelation of God's Word to pass on to future generations. Some of us just might.

I believe that God has something for all of us, but it may be much closer to home. I believe that God wants us first to love Him, to accept Him as the One and Only God, a God that is so merciful toward us that He sacrificed His only biological Son (metaphorically speaking) to open the door for us to become His adopted children.

I believe that God wants us to be happy, that He put desires in our heart, and that He thinks of us as He did Job. When talking about us, He may say something like, "Have you seen my son or daughter <insert your name>? I am so proud of him or her. I really like how he or she has lived their life."

God wants us to be happy accomplishing the things He put in our hearts. He gave us the mission to share the gospel of Jesus Christ, but for most of us, it is likely to be more related to the world we live in, and with the people we see regularly.

Let me get back to my original theme.

I am sure 50 is not too old. When I mentioned that I was having second thoughts about going back to school because I would probably be over fifty by the time I graduated, one wise friend responded, "You are going to be over fifty whether you go back to school or not. Go for it."

I often questioned myself, wondering if I was wasting my time. The answer is, "No." It has been more than twenty years since I earned my degree, and it has been well worth it. It is more than a piece of paper; it is a head full of knowledge that I didn't have before. I better understand life, know a little more about what I want to do, and have a greater determination to enjoy life to the end. In addition, it has kept me more employable.

Never underestimate the value of learning. Always be the one in your group who is soaking up all the knowledge you can. There are no boundaries around what your goals should be. Your desire may be to be a tournament fisherman, a charter boat captain, a nurse, a doctor, to regularly break par on the golf course, to be the smartest grandmother a child has ever hugged, and the list is endless. If you want it, God must have put it in there, go for it.

By the time you read this, our daughter, Terri, will have received her bachelor's degree from The University of Alabama. It has been exciting watching and cheering for her to complete her studies. She is about to embark on the next phase of her life.

I have more to say about different stages of life in these articles and end with something really special looking back at age 20, a time in life when many of us first believe we are failures.

NOTES

Part Three–Sixties

Let us continue with the theme, "When are we too old?"

I have determined that it is not 60. I have already been there and done that, and I don't see any signs of letting up now. Why do I spend my time writing and participating in other groups? Because I still feel young, and I want to make a difference in my own life, and one of the best ways to do that is to make a difference in the lives of others. I know only a few people may read this, but if one person reads it and is encouraged, it is worth it for me. If that person sends a note of encouragement back to me, then I have received a double portion from God.

Let me get back to the subject at hand. Consider Gilbert Morris, a well-known author of Historical Christian Fiction, who published his first book when he was well into his fifties. It seems that he just whetted the appetite of his readers for more. In order to meet their demand, Morris became a prolific writer, penning hundreds of books through his sixties, seventies, and into his eighties. The number of books he published is nearly three hundred. He wrote forty books in his "House of Winslow" series alone.

If you are in your sixties, stay active, do things <u>YOU</u> like and that <u>YOU</u> want to do. If you want to work. Do it. If you want to fish. Do it. The main thing is, do not sit and do nothing, and do not let others tell you what you want to do.

I do recommend that you get up every morning, get dressed, whether you plan to go anywhere or not, and make a difference in someone's life. If you are in this age group you may remember Jimmy Durante singing in his raspy voice, "Make someone happy, just one someone happy, and you will be happy too."

NOTES

Part Four–Seventies & Eighties

We are considering at what age we should say, "This is it. I don't need to believe I can accomplish anything of value in life. Maybe it's time for me to sit down and let others do for me."

I know health affects us more and more as we get older, and if we are bed-ridden or wheelchair bound, our mobility limits our going and doing. If we find our self in one of these situations, we understand that we may not be able to go. However, we still have some control over our own happiness. We still can encourage others. We can choose to offer kindness to those we are around.

If you are in your seventies, eighties, or older, still have most of your mental capacity, still have some physical mobility, and can communicate with others, you can make a tremendous difference in this world we live.

Consider Sister Lola, a widow of a Mississippi Pastor, an encourager to Carolyn and me, always active, happy, and fun to be around We only saw her once a year at a writer's conference. She was in her late seventies when we met her. She taught piano several days a week and loved to write encouraging words for everyone she met. She remained active in both her mind and body.

Ms. Lola passed away a few years ago, but my mind often flashes a vivid picture of her beautiful face and warm smile just to remind me of someone who made a difference. Her excitement with life always revived in me a spirit of determination to go on and to be more like her.

One day, and we don't know when that day will be, we will take in our last breath on this earth. Until that day, love those who God brings into your life, forgive those who choose to abandon you, and make a difference wherever you are.

Please accept my words of encouragement for you as I am reminded of how far God has brought me.

NOTES

Part Five–Nineties

How old is too old?

It was Wednesday night January 12, 1994, and we had just finished a scrumptious dinner at the University Club complete with a most wonderful ice cream desert, almond balls. Dr. Harriet Cabell went around the room introducing each of the staff members and teachers that worked closely with The External Degree program at The University of Alabama. When she got to Professor Colgan H. Bryan, she paused and emphasized to us that if we need a science, his *Engineering: The Foundation of the Modern World* course will be one of the most enjoyable learning experiences we will ever have.

I kind of passed over that, seeing that he was a frail looking man of 84 years old, and I was not sure that he would live long enough for me to finish the class. I didn't need to miss any time from my studies.

So, I waited until I could wait no longer and then in 1997, I decided to take his class. Now Professor Bryan was 87 years old and I was 51. Dr. Cabell didn't stretch any truth about a wonderful learning experience. I was just sorry that I had not taken any of his classes earlier.

Why am I rambling on about something of seemingly little importance? Professor Bryan continued encouraging, teaching, and inspiring students in practical aspects of life and science until he was 95 years old. My life would not be complete if I had not met this humble man who joined the University of Alabama's Aeronautical Aerospace & Engineering department in 1942 and headed up The University's efforts to support engineering and training for The United States of America during WWII. He was chairman of the department from 1952 – 1968. Thank-you, Professor Bryan for continuing to teach until I finally decided to learn.

Consider another person whose work inspired me.

I love to listen to books on tape/CD and I always have several in my truck. I listen to inspirational messages a good bit but most often I listen to fiction.

One day I picked up "The Lawgiver" on CD from the Mobile Public Library. I didn't know how good it would be, but other books written by Herman Wouk that I have read were wonderful. I checked out "The Caine Mutiny" from the library at Vigor High School in 1963, thoroughly enjoyed it, and wrote a passable book report on it. The book was later made into a movie starring Humphrey Bogart as Captain Queeg. I still remember the dastardly plot of the missing strawberries.

Wouk also wrote the books that were the basis for the two series on TV in the 1970's, "Winds of War" & "War and Remembrance."

Why would I say anything about this now? It is easy; Herman Wouk wrote "The Lawgiver" at the young age of 97.

Who can forget George Beverly Shea from the Billy Graham evangelistic crusades? Shea passed away on April 16, 2013 at the age of 104.

Do you remember George Burns the cigar-puffing comedian who along with his scatterbrained wife, Gracie Allen, entertained us from the early days of TV until he was 100? He often said (loosely quoting), "My doctor tells me to quit smoking these cigars or they will kill me. I buried my sixth doctor last week."

If you are not old, do you have some older people in your family? Take time with them. They have a lifetime of experience that they are likely to share. You will be amazed at what you learn.

Please do not ever just sit down permanently and do nothing. Continue to be active, do something. Contribute where you can. You will leave a lasting legacy.

NOTES

Part Six–Twenties

Have you really screwed up your life? Do you think that you are an utter failure?

I have written five articles to encourage readers to live life to the end always expecting a good outcome and to never give up. Today, I have a few words for those who may be at the front end of adulthood, and already feel defeated.

I am going to share a true story about the wisest and most loving person I know.

To this day she questions the wisdom of her parents, who when she was barely fifteen years old, sanctioned her marriage to a boy who was nearly twenty.

Her first child was born as she reached the ripe old age of seventeen and a half, her second child only fourteen months later. Within a year, not quite twenty years old, two children under three, a cruel and loveless husband, and her marriage of almost five years is falling apart. What does she do?

A simple letter from her mother opened reality to her. She didn't have a telephone and her mother had never written to her before. She sat on the back steps and cried as she read her mother's words. A first cousin, just six years older than her had been asleep in his bunk on the USS Forrestal off the coast of Vietnam. An accident on deck sent a raging fire through the ship killing him and 133 other sailors.

At the young age of 26, he was gone forever. What if she lived only until she was 26?

With mostly heartache over the realization her marriage was only going to get worse, she decided it was time to end it. Being a dedicated Christian, she knew that this was not the life God intended for any of us. She knew divorce was not God's ideal, but because her spouse chose to harden his heart toward her and the children, instead of asking God for the kind of Love they deserved, divorce became her answer.

Consider an inept local attorney who took care of the legal paperwork and convinced the judge to reward her exit from the marriage, with the Kenmore washing machine and eighty dollars a month to care for her two children. Then her ex-husband chose to leave the state to avoid paying that paltry sum, because he didn't want his ex, living a lavish life off any of his money.

Five years gone; she is back with her parents in a worse state than when she left. Less than a high school education, two kids who depend on her for everything, and she doesn't even have a car to drive to a job. Maybe it's time to give up.

Not her. God put His faith in her "As a grain of mustard seed," and instilled in her a strong desire to succeed. She didn't know how God would do it, but better days were coming.

Fast forward fifty years, a loving husband, a third child, five grandchildren and a lifetime of wisdom to share.

Please understand, there are relatively few things you can't recover from. Trust in God, and don't give up. God will make a way where there is no way.

NOTES

Wayne Brady

JOY OF LIFE

S tories for us to remember how much fun we have in life, with a few spiritual truths sprinkled in. There are many people, and a plethora of events that have shaped and molded us. Here are a few that shaped me.

Papa Fix It

My daughter, Tammi, once said, "Dad must have saved our family about a million dollars in household repairs."

I admit that I can fix many things, and I enjoy working around the house, but a million dollars in savings is an exaggeration. However, the importance of my skills and the resulting value to our family was made quite clear one Sunday afternoon.

When Tammi married, she and her husband frequently called on me to help with home improvements and maintenance in their household. Her three girls, six-year-old Brady, and two-year-old twins Courtney and Whitney have grown up watching Papa fix many of the broken objects that they have seen during their short lives.

Just a week earlier, the girls had stood patiently by my side as I disassembled, spliced, and reassembled The Great Mouse Detective videocassette. They then hugged me happily while telling their mother, "Papa fixed it, Papa fixed it," as the video began playing.

On this special Sunday afternoon, I was resting comfortably on the sofa, my mind drifting back and forth between the NASCAR race on television, and bream fishing on Bashi Creek with Little Granddaddy, Carolyn's dad, when the telephone rang.

Tammi said, "I want you to know these girls insisted that I call you."

"What's going on?" I asked.

"They were watching The Little Mermaid when the power on our street went off," Tammi continued.

I could hear the twins in the background saying, "Papa fix it, Papa fix it."

Tammi continued, "I told them that you couldn't fix this problem, but they wouldn't hear me. They kept insisting that I call you, that you could fix it. What do you want me to tell them?" *I could hear the concern in her voice. This event could make me human to her children. I would no longer be superman.*

My analytical mind raced. *What do I say? Will I have to admit to the girls that I can't walk on water, that there are some things I can't fix? What would I say if this were the plant supervisor calling with a similar problem? I can't say that.* Words formed in my mind and I was about to speak, when I heard Courtney and Whitney shouting in the background, "Papa fixed it, Papa fixed it."

Tammi said, "I want you to know the power just came back on. The girls took off to get back to Ariel. Somehow, you have just been saved. They believe you fixed it."

"I'm certainly not going to tell them anything different," I said. "Some days I would rather be lucky than good."

"I guess you are," Tammi said. "Let me go start the video."

"Okay, bye. We'll talk later," I said.

I hung up the telephone just in time to watch Dale Earnhardt win the race. I laid back on the sofa and thought; *I am lucky, so very lucky. It is a wonderful feeling to have someone who believes in me. Super Papa for a little while longer.*

NOTES

The Doorknob Speech

I do not write this in any kind of disrespect for my wife. Carolyn is a wonderful person that I love very much, but sometimes we conflict on a few certain things. It seems she has some privileges that I don't.

Take for instance the freedom to hang clothes on doorknobs. She can get by with it, I can't. It's just not an issue for her.

Our bathroom has two doors, one to enter, and a second one into the reading room. I like to close the doors when I go in, first for privacy and, secondly, to keep the light from shining in her eyes if she is still getting her beauty rest. However, on occasions, when I push a door it swings part of the way closed and then springs back open. It shouldn't do that, it's just an ordinary house door.

What's the problem? The doorknob has several layers of clothes; something she has recently worn, and then gently fitted around the knob to keep handy. If I mess with it, the stuff begins to fall off, and then it becomes my responsibility to take care of the rumpled items.

I had often wondered how she could continue to do this, until one day I figured it out. She never heard *The Doorknob Speech*.

I saw the movie *The King's Speech*. In it, King George VI, the heir to the British throne, gave a speech on September 3, 1939 to reassure his people about the future as his nation was on the brink of war. It was a wonderful speech, but it did not move me nearly as much as a speech I heard some twenty years later.

The Doorknob Speech, spoken directly to me when I was about fifteen years old, changed me forever.

I grew up in a small three-bedroom apartment in Alabama Village. At the end of a short hall was an open area that was just large enough for a collection of doors, five to be exact. Three-bedroom doors, one-bathroom door, and one closet door cloistered closely together in what would have been walls had the area been larger. The doors allowed the family members to pass through into one of the aforementioned rooms, when open, or provided a little privacy when closed.

Because I was often too lazy to hunt a coat hanger, I got into the habit of hanging clothes that I may be planning to wear again on the inside of mine and my brother's bedroom doorknob. Apparently, that was acceptable, but it seemed to cause a problem for my daddy when I let my clothes wander out into the hall and onto the other doorknobs.

One night, after he got home from his second job of the long day, when all he wanted to do was take a bath, go to bed, and get some rest, I captured his full attention.

It probably would have been okay if there had been an item or two on my bedroom doorknob, maybe even the closet doorknob.

I believe he started preparing the speech when he opened his own bedroom door and knocked some of my clothes to the floor, and he finalized it when he returned to the bathroom, grasped the doorknob, and more of my clothes fell to the floor in a crumpled heap.

After the rather long speech (in my mind) that ended with him threatening to go to Bates Brother's store the next morning to buy a bunch of doorknobs, and then him promising to nail them all over my bedroom walls so I would have a place to hang my clothes. Had he been a man prone to violence, I believe he may have considered wearing out my behind for the first time in my life.

I thank God that my daddy was a peaceful man, but it was something about the words and the tone of his speech that got my attention that night. To this day, if I see a doorknob with clothes hanging over it, I think the owner of that garment didn't hear the speech, and then I remember fondly how I got the undivided attention of my daddy that night. Oh, how I wish I could see and hear him again.

My Secretary

This is the story of another most important person in my life.

Because I choose not to reveal the real names of the characters included in this story, please refer to the Definitions List below to understand each person's role in this mostly true version of the story.

Definitions:

Doofus—The project engineer assigned to this project. EE and I reported to Doofus

EE—The engineer in charge of the electrical engineering and design group

PA—The purchasing agent assigned to this project

PM—The project manager over this project. Doofus reported to PM

I am going back to a time long ago and far away when I worked in another office of misfit engineers and designers.

Setup: I was the lead for the instrument engineering and design group for this project. To say the least, it was a difficult project. We were designing an industrial manufacturing plant that would be built in another state. No matter how hard we tried, we could not keep up with the schedule, and we were always over budget. Both factors are job killers for managers, and for this project that included me.

Early on a Monday morning, Doofus called EE and me into his office. The first words out of Doofus' mouth were, "I am going to give you two guys a secretary."

"Why?" I asked. Since I had never had a secretary, and I always wondered why Doofus did what he did. I was more than a little suspicious.

Doofus said, "Well, she has been working for PA, and she can't do anything. She is always late getting his work done. She can't type a simple memo. She can't do any of the ordinary tasks that a secretary should be able to do. We want to fire her, but PA is way too busy to document her problems. We want you two guys to take her with you, watch her, and record all of her issues so we can get rid of her."

"Whose budget will she be on?" I asked, knowing I did not have any money to pay for a secretary.

"She is on PM's budget," Doofus responded. "He hired her. He knew her and wanted to help her."

"Does she have a computer?" I asked. Computers were scarce in those days and our group of eighteen engineers and designers had to share the ten that were assigned to us. I didn't believe a secretary would be of much value to our group, but an eleventh computer would certainly help.

"She comes with a computer, Doofus responded. "You guys set-up a place for her, and we will move her tomorrow."

EE and I left Doofus' office and headed back to ours.

EE said, "It should not take long for us to gather enough information for them to fire her."

I responded to EE, "I have never had a secretary, and I am not about to work to get my first one fired. I want to see if she can be of any value for us."

"You take her then," EE said. "I don't need the hassle right now anyway."

That is how I became the only discipline lead to ever have my own personal secretary.

What follows is as Paul Harvey would say, "The Rest of the Story."

The first thing I did when I got back to my office was to call a meeting to tell our group about her.

I said something like, "Good morning team. Tomorrow, we are getting our own secretary, assigned only to the instrument group. Doofus told me that she cannot do anything. He wants us to gather information, so they can fire her. I won't do that. She has been working for PA. He is very demanding and can be very tough on the people working for him. I want you guys to get to know her, find out what she can do, and see if she can do anything of value for us. If nothing else, she comes with her own computer, and we can use her computer to share with our group."

I met her the next morning. She was very nice but seemed a little stressed. She told me that she was a widow and that things had been tough for her lately.

She was grateful to PM for hiring her. She did mention that she had difficulty keeping up with PA.

I told her our group would be less demanding and should be a whole lot less stressful than her previous assignment. I also told her I wrote my own memos and communications, and that all she had to do was to make copies and distribute them to the recipients. I would do what I could to make her job easier, and that I would help her fit in.

Just a day or two later, one of the engineers came into my office, "Our secretary is great. She does everything that we ask of her. Did you know she has written a book?"

"Written a book?" I asked.

"Yes, ask her about it."

I did ask her about the book. She explained, her name was not the most prominent on the book, but she wrote most of it, edited all of it, and prepared it for publication.

It was not difficult to find the book in print. Albertson's, our local grocery store, had a copy on a shelf near the magazines and other books. The title of the book, "Mobile" in huge letters across the front of the brilliant glossy cover caught my eye. I bought it and reviewed it that night. "Mobile" told the story of business in our city. Three authors were listed, and my secretary's photo was on the inside flap.

At our group meeting the next day, I looked at my secretary and said to the group, "We have a celebrity in our midst," as I pulled out the book and showed it to them. "Our secretary is a published author. I am going to pass this book around for you all to see."

Every person ooh'd and aaah'd about the book, and our secretary beamed. You could tell we had touched a nerve with her, a good nerve, and her heart.

Our working relationship only improved over the next few months.

I liked having someone who could help our team complete our work, especially when she did not count against my budget. The rest of the team worked with her and shared the use of her computer.

Personally, she helped me with my writing. My reports, memos, requests for quotes, and other project specific writing all improved.

Initially, she only made copies of my memos and issued them. One day, she asked me if I would mind if she reviewed my memos. She promised to never change the meaning of anything I wrote. She would only look for ways to improve my writing.

I discovered she had earned a master's degree in English. She eagerly shared her knowledge of composition to help me improve mine.

She told me once, "You are a good writer, strong and decisive, and I enjoy reading your work."

To say that our group fell in love with our secretary was an understatement.

From the first day she started with us until her last, she performed flawlessly. She was such a pleasure to work with.

After about three months, she came to me and said, "I have been offered a job that I really would like to take, but I like working for you and in this group. The job would provide a place for me to live, and that would be good. I don't know if I am going to take it. Please, give me your opinion."

I looked her in the eye and responded, "I have never had a secretary assigned to me. This project will end soon, and this group will be split up and be reassigned to other projects. You will be laid off or assigned to another person to work for, and we don't know who that will be. If this job offer is something that would be good for you, please, take it. I appreciate all you have done for us and me specifically."

That quickly, I was returned to the real world of performing my own secretarial duties. I take no credit for helping my secretary fit in and survive the tough world of industrial engineering. The group of people I work with made life easy for me and all who worked with us.

Doofus never did ask what was taking so long for me to get information to fire my secretary, and it was good that he didn't. We had too many other issues that I disagreed with him on, and it would not have been good for him to challenge me on this one.

I thank God for sending a teacher to inspire me, if only for three months. Having this secretary was a life changing experience for me. I will never forget her, and her book will always maintain a conspicuous place on my bookshelf.

A Twisted Tale

In 1997, I took a physics class at Pensacola Junior College. I remember some truths I was taught in that class. For instance, I learned Sir Isaac Newton's first laws of motion, "A body in motion tends to stay in motion and a body at rest tends to stay at rest." These laws are used extensively by engineers today to design vehicles that transport people, material, and equipment. Newton is also recognized for many other findings.

Legend is that Newton, the son of a farmer, enjoyed eating fruit more than growing it. Early in life, he learned if he wanted a piece of fruit, he could either climb a tree and pull it, or he would have to wait for one to fall.

Newton determined there was an unseen force, called gravity, always pulling a piece of fruit downward, and when that force exceeded the resistance of the stem holding it to the tree, the apple was coming at him. Everyone knew that apples would eventually fall, but no one else was curious enough to ask the question, "Why?"

You already know about the law of gravity, but now I am going to reveal another law you likely have never heard of.

The law of extension cords is a phenomenon that most of us are aware of but has escaped scrutiny from the great scientists.

From time to time we all have to work with extension cords, but they can be a challenge, and often they will cause the proverbial preacher to want to cuss.

All we want is to extend electrical power a little farther, or provide power for a second device, but no, the extension cord just won't cooperate. It will not make it easy. While we are not looking, the cord may circle around a ladder's leg to cause chaos when we move it about a room, pulling items from above, dragging objects below, and then coming unplugged right in the middle of our project.

A single cord can inconspicuously wrap itself around a user's leg while the other end attaches to an immovable object. When we reach the limits of the cord, it will cause us to lose our balance and do some kind of weird dance to keep from falling. Even if we are not hurt, becoming king of the klutzes' is embarrassing. Maybe no one saw me.

God help you if you have to use two extension cords. The two will work together against you creating multiple problems. They will slither around like snakes in some sort of love making ritual, rolling around each other so tightly that it becomes nearly impossible to separate them. They will render both cords useless and destroy more than four times as many items as their single counterparts in their diabolical scheme to ruin your day.

Don't tell them, but I have figured out a good use for extension cords, just not for the purpose they were manufactured. Because extension cords cling to everything, take one along if you plan to climb a mountain. Securely wrap it around your waist leaving plenty of slack. It will be aggravating at times hanging on most everything you encounter, however if you happen to fall in a way that would otherwise mean certain death, the extension cord will reach out and grab any and everything on the way down, and you will not fall very far.

Technically, it will be trying to be its normal aggravating self, eager to trip you, but without a brain it will not realize it is helping you. It really would rather see you fall 5,000 feet to your death.

It's a wonder I have not hanged myself with one of these cords, and it would serve me right after calling them out. It is probably best not to antagonize them; they are enough trouble without any provocation.

Just one day after I wrote the above, I experienced a new twist to this story, literally.

I have been working to finish my writing room, a replica of Middle Bay Light. I built a scaffold so that I could safely reach the fifteen-foot height to the ceiling. Because it is so tall, and I get tired constantly climbing up, and crawling down after each task, I decided to take a jig saw up to my work platform with me. This allows me to make trim cuts to the boards I am installing without having to go down to the floor so often. Of course, the saw requires electricity which will be supplied by an extension cord. No problem. I pulled the cord up and passed the male end down to my wife to plug in.

Ready to work, except I plan to use a pneumatic hammer to fasten the boards to the ceiling. I move my air compressor to the porch and pull the required hose through the window of my office and up to the scaffold and climb back up.

In position, sitting just below the peak of the ceiling with a board in my lap, an air gun resting on my right knee and a jig saw on my left. I hold the board against the ceiling, mark it, pull it down, press it against the handrail of the platform, and cut. Then I lay the saw back on my leg, place the board against the ceiling, and lift the air gun. I successfully drive three nails into the board, but not without interference from the extension cord who has joined with the air hose to make completing this project as difficult for me as they can. Just five more boards to go.

The extension cord did all it could to misguide the saw toward my leg. It seemed so excited at the idea of my blood dripping from the ceiling like from a scene in some macabre Alfred Hitchcock movie. Somehow, I kept the blade pointed at wood instead of my precious flesh.

Not to be outdone, the hose tried to control the air gun in a desperate attempt to nail my hand to the ceiling. Wouldn't they have cheered at that scene; me hanging there, like a sacrifice to an ophidian god, blood covering my tools, and the last few drops trickling to the floor. The responding paramedics would just look up and say, "He should have known better than to take that extension cord for granted, and this fool thought he could use an air hose at the same time. God have mercy on his soul."

Tomorrow I will be back at it. I am not going to let an extension cord or air hose get the best of me. I hope.

NOTES

Evolution and the Rabbit's Tale

D o you know what event triggered the evolution of the rabbit from an animal with a long bushy tail to one who would forever be referred to as Peter Cottontail?

Joel Chandler Harris wrote about it during the middle of the nineteenth century.

In case you don't know who Harris is, he is the writer credited with penning stories that were likely conceived in the mind of a Georgia plantation slave who had incredible insight, but little formal education. Harris probably heard the stories over and over again until they became imbedded in his soul. Some of the most prominent characters he wrote about include a very cunning rabbit, a dumb acting bear, and a semi-foxy fox. He referred to them as Brer Rabbit, Brer Bear, and Brer Fox. He wrote of other characters as they appeared in his fictionalized animal kingdom.

Many of his books and stories have been banned because some have declared them racist. I personally don't know what all of the fuss is about but if it is because of the difference in the dialect of the slaves' common to that era and the young lad he is telling the stories to, then maybe we ought to consider modernizing the stories and removing the offending language. It is a shame that an entire generation has been denied the wisdom so brilliantly shared by a suppressed people.

One of my favorite stories offers a plausible explanation for the origin of the phrase, "Freeze your tail off." You might know that it includes fishing as a key component.

The story begins with the young lad interrupting the old man who is just beginning one of his tales with Brer Rabbit walking down the road shaking his long bushy tail.

"Everybody knows that rabbits don't have long, bushy tails," the youngster said.

After some discussion back and forth, the old man continues his tale just as Brer Rabbit encounters Brer Fox toting a nice stringer of fish. Brer Fox tells Brer Rabbit that he caught them down at the baptizing creek. Since in those days the rabbit had a tail similar to the fox, Brer Fox explained that he just lowered his tail into the water around dusk and waited there until morning. At first light he pulled his tail in and it was full of fish just hanging on. Brer Fox said that he threw the little ones back.

In a few minutes they part and Brer Rabbit goes home and picks up a bottle of something to drink and even though it is turning cold, Brer Rabbit heads out for the creek. Brer Rabbit finds a comfortable spot and lowers his tail into the water and there he sat thinking how cold he was. Eventually, morning comes and Brer Rabbit likely thinking of nothing but the fresh fried fish he will be having in a few minutes, tries to pull his tail out of the water. When he pulls again, the restraining forces give way. He turns to admire his catch and then realizes that he doesn't have any fish, but worse than that, he has no tail. He had pulled it clean off.

The little boy asked if all rabbits are bob-tailed because of Brer Rabbit and the old man explains, they all took after their paw.

As you can easily see, the rabbit's tail didn't evolve to nothing slowly over thousands of years. No, in one long cold night of fishing, his long bushy tail was gone forever.

The Uncle Remus stories were a very good source of entertainment for me when I was young, so much that I read them to our children and then to our grandchildren.

Just so you know, writing for me is like me being thrown into a briar patch, my briar patch, another Uncle Remus tale.

Reference: *The Favorite Uncle Remus* book of stories by Joel Chandler Harris (1845-1908) Copyright 1948, renewed 1976 by Houghton Mifflin Company

NOTES

Bogey and the Boxer

"The only thing that we have to fear is fear itself"—
Franklin D. Roosevelt.

Johnny, a local hero, Golden Gloves contender, successful in boxing rings and even better in a street fight or bar-room brawl, was as confident a person as I have ever met. He freely demonstrated some of his favorite moves for me.

I only saw him fight a couple of times, never in an organized match, only in the aforementioned bar-room settings. I am so thankful that I was never on the receiving end of one of his violent blows. I didn't run around with him, but we did cross paths socially at some of the local night spots such as the Stork Club, which was on Cottage Hill Road.

He liked fighting men who were bigger than him, the bigger the better, and he would do all to avoid a fight with someone who was near his size or smaller. I saw him lay out a man much larger than him who was bullying a smaller patron at a bar with just three quick punches. He would not back down from a fight even with multiple opponents, and he could take a punch from anyone, no matter how big or how strong his challenger.

He simply was not afraid of anyone.

Oops, I'm sorry, I nearly forgot to mention his one nemesis who could always strike terror in him. What kind of a man could shake his confidence? Only the least most unintimidating person that I ever met. They never faced off in a ring, nor did they trade blows on some dark alcohol filled night.

He should have been addressed as Mr. Fussell, but we were instructed to call him Bogey. I suspect he was named after the word that means just a little off, always one stroke away from par, the benchmark for any given hole in the game of golf. I assume that he was well liked, and that his friends chided him regularly about his substandard golfing skills. He was just the nice old man that Johnny and I both worked for, and he was probably younger then than I am now.

The year was 1964, and I had been hired right out of high school in the extruder plant at International Paper Company's Mobile mill.

Bogey and the boxer, as different as two people could be, worked together in the same department. They both ran things. Bogey managed the extruder plant and Johnny ran a re-winder that was used to take paper from huge rolls and transfer it to small cores that were more suited to customers' needs.

Some days it would take hours to repurpose a single roll for shipment and other days we would be running 9" diameter paper rolls that took less than a minute to spit out 20 or more rolls that were only a couple of feet long. The two extremes made for some interesting work shifts, the one waiting the entire day and maybe only transferring one roll, and the other wrapping non-stop for eight hours, and the backlog be greater when we got off work than when we started.

Johnny was a confident operator and seldom made mistakes. Even though he was shorter than me, he stood tall in front of his control panel as confident as a pilot about to maneuver his plane into combat. He just never wavered. Unless . . .

Bogey was a competent manager skilled in the art of paper making who knew how to motivate people. However, when it came to Johnny, Bogey sensed Johnny's trepidation when they were together. On busy days, he left Johnny alone to do his work in peace.

On slow days, Bogey's mischievous side got the best of him and he was compelled to break the boredom. Since none of the rest of us were intimidated in his presence, we were not very good candidates for his razzing.

We all knew when it was going to happen, because Bogey came through greeting each of us real friendly making sure we knew to be watching. On these special days, Bogey would eventually stroll nonchalantly up to Johnny and greet him also. He would then position himself directly behind the boxer who could have literally knocked his block off had he wanted to. Bogey would just stand there watching over Johnny's shoulder, both staring at the control panel. In a few moments Bogey would begin to rock back and forth on the heels of his spit-shined wing tips while continuing to watch the boxer's every move as skillfully as if he were sizing him up for a quick attack.

It would not be long before Johnny, the reluctant warrior, would exhibit a small sign of weakness, and with his confidence shaken a bit, he began to make bad decisions. It usually started with a slight twist of a control knob that did not need twisting. It would not be long before he just had to make another adjustment. There was no way that he could stand there and do nothing with this giant of a man watching.

Eventually, Johnny had made enough adjustments that the paper roll would begin to wobble. He turned another knob and then another until the paper roll vibrated so violently that the sheet would break, and be catapulted high in the air and then crumple back to the floor in an ever-increasing pile of wastepaper.

It was only then that Bogey would turn his back on his victim and stroll victoriously back to his office quietly collecting grins and high fives from everyone who had watched him torture the boxer for another round.

After Bogey had cleared the area, Johnny would turn to me and say, "I don't know why that man does that, he has to know how it affects me."

My response was always, "I don't know either," mustering all the strength I could to maintain a poker face.

More than fifty years and I remember it like it was yesterday. I saw Johnny a few years ago at a no-class reunion. He's aged and doesn't move as quickly as in those early years, but I knew better than to bring up the story that had embarrassed him so often, or to laugh at him.

God Bless You Old Friend.

NOTES

Chickasabogue: A Mystery

The swimming hole seemed so far away, but in fact it was less than 2 1/2 miles from our front door in Alabama Village, one of the housing projects that were built to provide places to live for the thousands of workers imported to support the shipbuilding industry during World War II. Chickasabogue creek, the closest navigable water to our home was an exploration frontier for some of us twentieth century Tom Sawyers who grew up in and around Prichard in the fifties and sixties.

Prichard was a wonderful place with lots of outdoor activities available to keep us younger folks occupied and out of trouble. The city maintained numerous recreation areas. The main one near city hall had a zoo with gorillas, monkeys, and alligators. There was also a playground with rides and swings, a baseball / football field that also served as an arena for rodeos, and a huge swimming pool for us to cool off and let loose some energy during the summer months.

It was a completely different era, an innocent time free from worry about trivial stuff like boundaries. If we could walk there, we could play as long as we wanted. If we were home in time for supper, we were within the limits our parents set.

If we wanted to go swimming when the Prichard Park swimming pool was closed, or we didn't have the ten cents required to pay for our admission, Chickasabogue Creek was our best alternative. The creek originated above Oak Grove and snaked several miles all the way to the Mobile River near the paper mills. There were several swimming holes along the way, with the main difference between each being the temperature of the water. The closer to the spring that fed the creek, the colder the water.

We were feeling the heat and humidity on this early summer day in 1965. Steve Ard and I had been swimming with others at the old Hollingsworth & Whitney site known by most as the H&W, when we decided to water ski for a while. I got in the boat and threw the rope to Steve. In just a few moments we were on our way. I maneuvered around the winding curves watching intently for oncoming boats with one eye and keeping Steve in the rear-view-mirror with the other. When we rounded the last tight bend in the river, I noticed someone in a thicket near the bank waving to us. I quickly pulled back on the throttle and dropped Steve into the cold black water.

As I turned the boat around and headed back to get Steve he asked, "What did you do that for?"

I pointed to the bank as I pulled him into the boat.

I turned the boat around and we headed toward the man who was dressed in a blue uniform complete with spit shined shoes. The patch on his shoulder read, "Saraland Police Department."

"Man am I glad to see y'all. I have been trudging through this swamp for two hours."

We helped him into the boat, and he explained why he was where he was.

"A lady up in Saraland called our office and said that she had heard shots fired, and someone yelling for help from out her back door down toward the south."

"My partner and I responded to the call. We heard the yelling also, but we weren't exactly sure where it was coming from. I drew the short straw and started on foot in the direction of the sounds, but I haven't seen anything suspicious. I was hoping I could find another way back to Saraland without having to go back through that swamp."

We ferried him to the launch ramp on the north side of the Highway 43 Bridge where he found a telephone and called the department for a ride back to Saraland.

After he left, Steve and I walked back to the dock where we had tied the boat. A man who was working on the motor in a boat that was tied nearby asked, "What was the policeman doing with you?"

I related the story the policeman had told.

A slight grin caused his lips to turn up slightly at the edges as he said, "I'll bet that was me."

He went on, "I had been sculling along fishing near the bank, caught a nice mess of bream. When it started to get hot and the fish had quit biting, I was ready to go home. I packed up my stuff and pulled on the starter rope time after time, but my motor wouldn't crank. All it would do is spit, sputter, and backfire. I pulled the rope again and again, but all it did was, 'Pop – Pop.'"

He continued, "I alternated between pulling on the rope and yelling, 'H-e-l-p, H-e-l-p.' Finally, another boater came along and towed me here."

I climbed into our boat. Steve untied us, stepped aboard also, and gave a slight shove. I said to Steve as we backed away from the dock, "I'll bet he is right. That's exactly what she heard."

Steve and I went back to playing and didn't worry anymore about the mysterious shooting on Chickasabogue Creek.

Thinking about it now, it probably would have made sense to call the police department and tell them the facts, but we didn't. We didn't normally go looking for policemen on purpose in those days.

NOTES

Ever Been Fired

Yesterday, I drove four hours for a meeting to only be fired shortly after it started. Technically, they didn't fire me, but it was obvious they didn't want me, and they seemed awfully happy when I offered my resignation from this non-paying assignment. I was just glad it happened early, so I could start the four-hour drive back home.

On the way home I remembered a similar incident that happened a long time ago.

I graduated from high school on a Thursday, and a friend talked me into riding over to International Paper Company the following Tuesday to put in an application for work. They called my home before I got back there and hired me the next day. They never called my friend even for an interview. I don't know why.

Fast forward nearly three years.

I was working as a pipe fitter helper in the group headed by Mr. Otto Smith. To say that Otto was grouchy would be a compliment. Example, one morning while taking a break, I had sat down and was eating a bologna sandwich when Otto walked by. He looked at me and said, "There ain't but one job in this department that requires a man to sit down and I already got it. You can eat standing up."

He didn't get any better than that.

Was he justified in his attitude toward me? Yes.

I worked rotating shifts doing preventative maintenance, and attending to operational problems that needed to be repaired quickly to keep the mill operating.

In my defense, I did know how to work and did a good job when I was there. The problem was that often I would start doing something during the day that affected my desire to be at work at night, especially on the graveyard shift on Friday or Saturday nights.

Because I was single and didn't have any real responsibilities, I often found myself at places I ought not to have been and drinking stuff that I should not have been drinking. More than a few young ladies posed as my mother and called the guards at the mill (while music blared in the background) to tell them I was sick and unable to come to work that night.

Larry Funk worked the shift just ahead of mine. He was married with young children who depended on him, so he got to work a lot of overtime covering my shifts.

I can honestly say I had never seen Otto Smith smile, not once. This day everything changed.

I walked into his office, he spun his chair around, and in his usual deep voice he bellowed, "What do you want?"

I said, "I am going to say something that will make you happy."

He looked puzzled as he said, "I doubt that."

I said softly, "I quit."

His scowl turned into a huge grin and he said, "I didn't think you would ever do anything to make me happy."

No, Otto didn't fire me, but he sure seemed awfully happy on that day more than fifty years ago. I know I was.

NOTES

Holy Moly

I do not remember the entire day, but a few excerpts will likely remain in my memory bank until they declare my brain, "Dead."

Sometime after dinner on that day, my stomach began to act up, felt like a pot boiling faster and faster. I didn't know what was going on, but the pain took over my body and controlled my every thought. Something had to be done.

A long story shortened, we wound up in the emergency room at Springhill Memorial Hospital.

With a nurse on one side of the gurney I was laying on, and a doctor approaching the other side, Carolyn eased out of their way and moved to stand at my feet.

Standing there, she patted my legs to comfort me. She looked down to where she had been touching, and then panned down to the bottom of my feet. I still had my shoes on. The look that descended over her face scared me. What did she know? What did they tell her? What did she see that I didn't? In a millisecond, I knew.

As inconspicuous as possible, she reached down and eased my shoes off my feet and hugged them close to her breast. Even as she flashed a sigh of relief, I knew that this was not going to be good. I remembered there were quarter-size holes in those shoes when I had put them on that morning. I had replaced the cardboard on the inside to prevent my sock feet from touching the ground.

The look that transmitted displeasure with me soon vanished, replaced by one of pure horror, as she looked down to see my big toes staring up at her like a pair of popped weasels. They seemed to be mocking her. She grabbed those ragged white socks and snatched them off one at a time. She looked around to make sure no one had seen her, or worse yet, to ensure they had not seen my overused shoes and socks.

The doctor finished his examination, wrote a prescription that he said would ease my pain and eventually heal me, and quietly dismissed himself.

After I had been discharged, and we were sitting in the car, before Carolyn touched the ignition to start the car, she turned and looked at me. There was no smile on her face, and no humor in her voice as she said, "We will get that medicine after we go by Shoe Station."

I have heard all my life that I should always wear clean underwear in case I am ever in an accident. Nothing was ever said about my shoes or socks.

Later that evening, our daughter called from her home in Chicago. What did Carolyn share about our trip to the hospital? Nothing about the sickness that sent us there. No, she shared the near-death experience I almost encountered when she saw me wearing those shoes and socks after their life had long ago abandoned them.

I guess I just embarrassed her. Not the first time, and I am sorry to say not the last.

NOTES

A Small World

Saturday, June 4th, 1955 summer vacation from school studies was officially here. I had completed all requirements to be promoted to the fourth grade at Ellicott Elementary School in Chickasaw, Alabama just the day before. The anticipation of the day-long activities I was going to enjoy was all that was on my mind.

I had few worries and knew nothing about a series of nuclear explosions the United States had detonated in the Nevada desert during the previous three months. It would be fifty-five years before I would meet Roy Dobbs, a young U. S. Air Force enlisted man who witnessed fourteen of the explosions at close range that spring as part of Operation Teapot.

At school, we participated in local air raid drills and every once in a while, we would evacuate the buildings, load in cars driven by parents, fall in line as directed, follow the police escorted entourage, and travel way out in the country hoping to minimize casualties from a possible enemy attack. WWII was still fresh on everyone's mind, and the way it ended put fear in the hearts of many Americans.

This day began as most others, with my brother, Donnie, and I locked in a competitive battle to see who was better at something, and it didn't matter what.

Six months earlier Santa Claus had brought me a brand new 24" Western Flyer bicycle and Donnie the 26" version of the same bike.

The smaller diameter tires on my bicycle gave me a distinct acceleration advantage over my three-year-older brother whose bigger tires required much more power to get up to speed. I used that advantage to take an early lead down Dallas Street. Just fifty yards before the end of the street, I maintained a comfortable lead, and victory would soon be mine. I caught a glimpse of Donnie out of the corner of my eye. He was pedaling as fast as he could in a desperate attempt but with little chance of catching me when my pedals went limp. No resistance to my frantic pedaling, no increase in speed, but worse than that, no brakes.

In an attempt to avoid speeding onto heavily travelled (not) Chilton Street, I swung the handlebar to the right. Aw man, that stop sign is just too close. I turned the handlebar even more to the right, and most of the bicycle cleared the post except. . .

My left pedal hooked the signpost and the post held fast. In fact, that concrete post would have stopped a '55 Chevy in its tracks and sent the driver hurtling through the windshield.

Hooking the post as I did would have been okay if my bare foot had not been on the pedal. In an instant the cutting pain shot through me as the bicycle whipped around and threw me to the ground

I just sat there and stared at my foot. The skin was folded way back. Not much blood, but I saw things that I should not be seeing. I saw something move as I wiggled my toes. Later I learned they were ligaments.

Doggone terrible way to lose a race. Donnie did come back, lay his bicycle down, and help me walk home.

A whirlwind of new experiences began for me right then.

When my daddy saw what had happened, he wrapped a white towel around my foot, picked me up, and placed me in the middle of the front seat of the family's '54 Ford. Our next-door neighbor got in on the right side and held me during our trip to the Mobile Infirmary. I had been to that hospital two years earlier when my sister was born, but I was not allowed inside then. On that day we children had to stay outside so we ran and played on the grass in front of the hospital waiting for our daddy to come back.

This day I remember lying on a hospital bed and the technician telling me that he was giving me something to help me sleep. He said, "Count backwards starting at a hundred."

100, 99, 98, 97, 96, 95, 94, 93 . . . is all that I remember.

The next thing I knew was waking up Sunday morning in a room with a stranger in the next bed. I believe his name was James. He was much older than me. I learned that he had dove into shallow water, cracked some bones in his neck, and suffered some paralysis in his body.

After the doctor made his round, Daddy paid the hospital $29.50 cash to cover the bill I had run up and took me home.

That was the beginning of a difficult summer for me. My foot was in a cast and I had to use crutches to help me walk. I remember going on summer outings with the family and sitting on the creek banks as the other children frolicked in the water.

When they removed the cast and started changing the bandages regularly the skin on my foot went through several disgusting color changes before it finally settled in to baby pink just in time for school to resume.

I was so thankful when my foot was almost fully restored, and I could return to school. That year I met two new friends, Bobby Williamson and Eugene Elmore, who I remain close with today.

Wow, 63 years have passed, and that scar is still with me, a stark reminder of a physical injury that healed long ago. I only wish emotional injuries could heal so completely.

For some reason, my mother kept a copy of the itemized hospital bill my daddy had paid. I saw it the other day: Operating Room - $10.00, Drugs - $5.50, Hospital Room - $8.00, Drugs $2.00, and Drugs $4.00.

Wow, how things have changed.

A SOB Story

There have been a lot of important people in my life. This is the beginning of friendships with two men who helped me transition from a craftsman in industrial plants to a manager of contract engineering services.

The year was 1988. The first one had hired me to work for him at Brown & Root in their Mobile, Alabama engineering office just a week before I met the second one.

I was sitting at my drafting table, head down, checking an instrument drawing when I noticed him out of the corner of my eye. He entered the area and walked straight into L. D.'s office with an air of authority. Since no one was in there and I was the closest person to him, he turned to me and asked, "Do you know where he is?"

He didn't fit the mold of managers or other engineers that I had met. His clothes didn't say, "I am somebody important." In fact, they didn't say anything at all. His shirt was multicolored like those my mother used to buy for me each August, at the Fair Store in Prichard, to wear for the following year. They were nice but not much different from the other 700 or so boys in my high school.

I responded, "No sir I don't, but he should be back shortly."

He said, "When he comes back, would you ask him to come see me?"

His wavy gray hair and his confident tone implied that he was somebody important to this office and to this project in particular.

"Yes sir, who may I say came by?"

The warm smile that broadened his face belied his words, "Tell him the old son-of-a-bitch came by." He then turned and walked away.

Some may say, "You shouldn't use that term in your writing," and I am uncomfortable writing it. I hope that after you read this story, you will understand why it is important to state it exactly as it was said. Please forgive me. Generally, people in professional offices don't use vulgar language.

My boss, L. D. Pee, soon returned and I called out to him as he turned to go into his office. "Someone came by to see you," I said.

L. D. turned to me and asked, "Who was it?"

"He didn't give me his name. He only said, 'Tell him the old son-of-a-bitch came by.'"

L. D. smiled, kind of chuckled and said, "I know who he is," and quickly turned and headed in the direction of the SOB.

On this day more than thirty years ago, we three began a lifelong friendship. The two of them contributed so much to me and my life both, professionally and personally.

L. D. Pee taught me engineering and project management for the next fifteen years. I told him once that he was the second-best boss I had ever worked for.

"Second best? He asked.

"Yeah, George has passed on now. I can't move a dead friend from his position. Now if you want to die, I may move you to #1."

Dinty Walston, who was anything but an SOB, is the best project manager I have ever known. Time has not dimmed the importance of his expertise in my life.

To say that I loved these two men, would be a gross understatement.

NOTES

Hello Handsome

I remember it like it was yesterday. It was not yesterday. It was 1990.

I stopped at the project secretary's desk in the double-wide construction trailer where we were building a huge new addition for a specialty chemicals company in Shreveport, Louisiana.

I flashed one of my everyday smiles and said, "Good Morning, Betty."

"Hello handsome," Betty replied.

I turned to look and see who might be standing behind me and was surprised when no one was there.

As I turned back to Betty, she said, "You don't take compliments well, do you?"

"I don't get them often," I replied.

"I don't believe that," Betty said.

I went on to my office with a little spring in my step and soon forgot Betty's words.

Years later, I remembered this conversation. Still no-one else had used the word, "Handsome," in reference to my looks, not even my wife.

Because I wore super thick horn-rimmed glasses in my earlier days. Some friends called me, "Mr. Magoo" after the lovable, but nearly blind cartoon character brought to life by the voice of Jim Backus. Before that, a few just called me, "Four-eyes."

Oh, don't feel sorry for me. I didn't take offence hearing such comments. I had enough friends, and I learned to take good-natured kidding, even if it was not meant in kindness. I knew I was average and accepted it. Average intelligence, average athletic ability, and average looks. Typically, average served me well. I could easily fade into the background and become invisible in nearly any setting.

I told this story to someone recently and received this response, "She was just flirting." My interpretation of this lady's comment; she didn't mean it literally. So, not even once in my life had anyone called me handsome and meant it.

Well it felt good for 27 years, but that was snuffed out a few weeks ago.

After hearing me refer to this encounter a while back, my wife stated that she would not have fallen for an ugly person, and, in fact, she did believe that I was, "Handsome."

Thank you, beautiful lady.

Now, the beautiful lady calls me, "Handsome." Yes, it feels good.

NOTES

Mississippi One Tale

I had the privilege of growing up around a lot of loving people. No, I don't remember any of them ever telling me they loved me, but clearly their actions reflected it. Most all of them had time to make a little boy feel special; from the biscuits the women baked just to see me devour them, to the stories they would tell as they watched my enraptured facial expressions.

I love to share the stories that thrilled me so long ago, as they settled into secret places in my inquisitive mind. Here's one from a favorite uncle of mine, Uncle Elmer Duvall.

Uncle Elmer served at sea with the U. S. Navy during World War II and rambled around the United States for as long as I knew him. He worked all sorts of jobs; rough-necking on oil rigs, sailing as a merchant marine, and waiting tables in posh restaurants in New Orleans to name a few. He never married and never owned much. I really loved him and was especially mindful when he was around. He loved his baby sister, Maggie, my mother, and frequently visited in our home.

One memorable story that he told me in private was of an encounter with a young man shining shoes on the streets of the Crescent City.

He had just finished watching the youngster spit polish his shoes to a shine that would have made the captains of the ships he had served on proud. Uncle Elmer liked to dress well, and those shoes gave him a look that pleased him this day.

He lifted himself up from the makeshift box that the boy used for his customers to sit on, pulled change from his pocket, poured it carefully into his left hand, sorted around, pulled out a shiny new dime, handed it to the boy, and said, "Much obliged, son."

The young man grinned as his eyes focused on the remaining change in Uncle Elmer's hand, "Thank you, Sir."

As Uncle Elmer turned to walk away, the little guy spoke up, "Excuse me Sir."

Uncle Elmer turned and returned the boy's gaze, "Yes son, what can I do for you?"

The boy really wanted that bright silver quarter that stood out from the other coins that had been in Uncle Elmer's hand just a few seconds ago.

"Mr. Elmer, for that case-quarter you have, I will tell you where you got your shoes, I will tell how many children your father had, and I will tell you what state you were born in."

Intrigued, Uncle Elmer listened carefully to his challenger's words. Now, how could this young man possibly know these three facts about me? No one around here knows that much about me.

"Ok son, you have a deal. Tell me where I got my shoes?"

"That's easy he said, you got your shoes on your feet."

Uncle Elmer thought a second and said, "You're right about that. Now, tell me how many children did my father have?" Very few knew that fact seeing that Uncle Elmer's father had been married before he married Elmer's mother, and there were fourteen children between both wives.

"Your father didn't have any children, your mother had 'em all."

Uncle Elmer thought again and said, "I can't argue with your logic there; now tell me what state was I born in?"

"That's the easiest question of all, you were born in the state of infancy," he said grinning.

"Okay, you win." Uncle Elmer smiled, pulled out that shiny new case-quarter that hardly had time to cool since he had received it as part of his wages just a short time ago, and flipped it to the youngster.

It didn't bother Uncle Elmer at all that an eleven-year-old had just hornswoggled him.

When Uncle Elmer related the story to me, he was very clear that he had a lot of respect for that young entrepreneur.

Thank you, Uncle Elmer Duvall, for sharing your life and tales with me.

NOTES

What's the Score?

"Why don't you come and watch us play ball tonight?" George asked.

"Ball, what kind of ball?" I replied.

"Softball, company team, we play at Sage Avenue Park at 7:30. Bring your family. It's a lot of fun."

"A lot of people come?" I asked.

"Sure, many employees and their families. You will enjoy it."

I thought, it may be a good way to get to know my co-workers better, so I replied, "We'll try to make it."

I had only been working at Virginia Chemical three months and I wanted to fit in.

"The games only last an hour, so don't be late," George said.

We arrived at the ballpark at 7:00 P.M. The stands were already full of fans cheering for their teams.

George met us as we approached the stands, and with a big ole smile, he said, "Welcome, Wayne. I assume this is your family."

After introductions, George said, "The stands will empty as soon as this game is over. Y'all will be able to find a seat then."

As co-workers and their families arrived, I methodically introduced my wife and children to them. After about ten minutes, the stands erupted into a joyous victory celebration. Soon they began picking up their stuff and exited to meet with their players. We climbed to our seats and repopulated the stands. Carolyn and I took a top row seat while Tammi, Terri, and Gary ran around and played with other children.

Marla, the plant secretary, and her husband sat about four rows in front of us. Willie Byrd sat just to our left, and others filled the stands all around us.

About ten minutes before game time, George, who is the manager of the softball team, climbed the stands, stopped right in front of me, and said, "We do not have a score keeper. Will you serve as ours?"

Now, I played a little softball at PE while in school and I understood the basics of the game. I had also seen the Little Rascals play ball on TV, and I understood basically they wrote a number on a chalk "score board" after a runner crossed home plate. They also kept track of how many outs a team had.

"Will the other team be okay with this? I asked.

"Sure. Sure. There is an official scorekeeper for the game. I just need someone to keep up my lineup book and keep track of the game for me. I will use it to review the game tomorrow," George said.

"Okay, I'll do it."

"Good," George said as he sat down beside me. "Have you ever done this before?"

"No," I said.

"Let me show you a few things," George said as he opened a spiral bound notebook. "This is an official lineup book. It's where I want you to record everything. I have already filled in the starting lineup. We will substitute some players around the third or fourth inning."

I nodded, thinking it looked innocent enough. I would soon learn there was more to it than I initially thought. A lot more.

George pointed to a square on the page and said, "If a batter hits a line drive, draw a straight line from home plate to the location where the ball is fielded." George drew an arrow from home plate on the little diamond to a point just to the right of second base. "If the second baseman catches it then put 01 in the box. If he catches a bouncing ball, then throws it to first for an out then draw 4—3 like this and put 01 in the box. Now, if he misses the ball and the batter gets on base because of the missed ball enter E1 in the box. If the second baseman catches the ball and throws it to first base but it's not in time to get the runner out, then it's a base hit and enter 1B in the box."

If all this was not enough, "If the batter pops the ball up, draw a line like this," George continued as he penciled a steep arc from home plate to second base. "If it is a low fly ball make the arc less pronounced, like this." He drew a slightly less curved arc from home plate to second base.

"Wow, there is more to this than I thought," I said feeling overwhelmed with what he had shown me so far.

"Yes, it is. Do you have any questions?" George asked.

"Yes, I do," I responded. "Why did you enter the 4—3 right there?"

"Because the number 4 player, the second baseman, made the out by throwing the ball to the number 3 player, the first baseman."

He continued, "All of the players on the field are numbered. The pitcher is number 1, the catcher number 2, the first baseman number 3, the second baseman number 4, shortstop number 5, the third baseman number 6, the left fielder number 7, left center field number 8, right center field number 9, and the right fielder number 10. Numbering the players makes it easier to keep up with who is doing what."

This is going to be much more complicated than I thought. Feeling a little like being in an Abbott and Costello conversation, I asked, "Who's on first?"

"Three," George said and then smiled, "You got it."

"I tell you what, I'll stay up here with you during the first inning until I have to bat, and help you get started," George said.

"Thanks, I'd appreciate that."

"No, thank you for helping," he said.

It was helpful to have George with me during the first inning. Our first batter hit a little looper over second base into right center field. The fielder had no chance to get him out at first, so I put 1B in the box. The next batter hit a line drive to the shortstop, and he threw the ball to the second baseman to get the advancing runner out. The second baseman turned and fired the ball to first.

"Safe," Russell Osborne, the league hired umpire, yelled as he waved his hands in a motion that apparently also meant safe. I wrote 1B in the block for the hitter.

George looked at what I had done and then said, "No, that was not a base hit. It was a fielder's choice, because the shortstop could have gotten the batter out if he had thrown to first, but he chose instead to get the lead runner at second. So, you enter FC and not 1B."

"I see," I said kind of mumbling half understanding.

"Now you have to go back to the previous batter's box and modify it to show out number 01 by a throw from the shortstop to the second baseman like this 5—4.

"Is all this necessary?" I asked.

"It most certainly is. With a properly documented score book I can review the game completely and better understand how well our players are doing. This is a very key function. I've got to go but I'll check back with you the next time we are at bat. Do the best you can.

The game moved quickly, and George did check with me occasionally, answering questions and correcting mistakes. He kept reassuring me. I really got it mixed up when we substituted players.

After about thirty minutes, Marla turned to me and asked," What's the score?"

"Six," I said.

"Six?" She asked.

"Yes, six," I said again.

"Shouldn't it be six to something or something to six?" She asked.

"No, just six." I could feel every eye in the stand staring at me now, asking the same question.

"Who has six?" Marla asked.

"We do."

"What does the other team have?"

"I have no idea. It took all I could do to keep up with our team. I spent most of the time they were batting correcting my mistakes."

Marla turned to the rest of the crowd and said, "The score is six!"

NOTES

LET'S WRITE

Lessons to inspire you to record your thoughts and ideas. You are important, and what you say is significant. This is not designed to be a full-fledged writing course. They are only a sampling of the writing discipline to help you get started.

Want to Write?

Now go, write it before them in a table, and note it in a book, that it may be for the time to come for ever and ever: (Isaiah 30:8 KJV)

Have you ever thought you had something to say? Do you believe your opinion is as important and correct as the next person's? Are you a little apprehensive to share it? Maybe at some point in your life you were belittled, or your comments were dismissed as irrelevant.

I am not asking these questions in some money-making scheme. No, I want to encourage you to speak up and reach out with your words. You may believe that you lack the skills to share confidently, but please, let me assure you that you are better equipped than you may believe. You have a lifetime of experience and have overcome most of the problems you have encountered; often it may have been in the school of hard knocks.

Most often, we learn by trial and error. If we try something, fail the first time and give up, then we do not learn. However, most of us are challenged when something we want resists our desire to achieve it. Those challenges make us stronger and more determined to succeed. I could share story after story from my own life, where it would have been easy to give up and settle for something less than what I want, something less than God's best for me. However, my head is just hard enough to resist attempts to stunt me when I really want something, or if I really believe that I am right. Reread an earlier story in this book, *You are Important.*

Please, let me encourage you to open your heart and let out what's inside. If you are apprehensive, ask me and I will share with you what I know.

In this section, I share some thoughts and ideas from my limited inventory to encourage you to write. I pray, they will spark something inside you to get your creative juices flowing. Write from your heart about things that are important to you. Don't expect miracles, but receive honest advice from someone who earlier would not share anything except with a few close friends.

God Bless You and Happy Writing.

NOTES

Write the Basics

If you want to write, you want to write something worth reading. You only have to master a few basics. You don't have to go back to school for years, but you may have to learn a few rules, and develop some new skills. My English 101 teacher encouraged me with the following words, "You don't make every mistake there is in writing, only a few. You conquer those few and you will be on your way." She was right about me, and I believe it will be the same for you.

I was talking with a friend one day who said, "I don't want to waste my time learning how to write, I just want to write." This statement was from a born-again Christian who had learned some truths from God, and believed he was the only one who could share them. He justified his decision not to begin studying the craft of writing, because he believed the Lord would return before he finished any studies. Of course, he was wrong. If Jesus returns before we complete a task, we win.

My opinion, if God gives us something to say, He wants us to use the words that will accomplish His intended purpose. We must have the skills to develop a compelling and well-written article.

Consider the following simple illustration.

I worked at Tom's Dairy Freeze in Prichard, Alabama during my senior year of high school. One of the most difficult skills that Tom required every employee to master was to make a perfect soft serve cone of ice cream, a staple for his business. We had two sizes.

The nickel cone was normally purchased by parents of small children who could not be expected to handle a really tall swirl of the sweet treat. For this size, all I had to do was hold the handle of the ice cream dispenser down and start filling the cone from the bottom, and then make a small swirl as the creamy goo extended above the sides of the crunchy cone. This was a piece of cake, pretty easy to make.

The ten-cent cone was another story. The goal was to fill the cone from the inside up the sides and produce a perfectly symmetrical swirl that extended as high as possible, with each pass a little smaller than the last, until all there was room for was a small point. The higher the mound, the happier the customer.

As teenage fry cooks, we competed for the mythical "Perfect Cone Maker" award. Our goal was for customers to come in and say, "I want a ten-cent cone of ice cream and I want Wayne to make it." Nothing was more disheartening for me than to take an order, and have the customer request, "I want Kenny to make it."

I am reminded how important it is to develop the art of cone building when I drive-through a McDonalds and be handed a cone that doesn't contain much ice cream at all. Even worse, is to have it full, but leaning heavily to one side, threatening to fall into my lap

I said all of this to say our writing should accomplish the same goal. We want people to be eager to read something we wrote.

Our writing should start well, and continue to shape a story perfectly, like out of a cone until it reaches a perfect end. If it is topped off with special meaning like "a cherry," they are really happy.

Let me encourage you to learn to fill a cone, maybe make some nickel ones for a while, and then continue improving your confidence, until you can build a tasty story that is a sweet savor for your readers.

Don't let my babbling scare you. I will share some ideas on how to start and I am always open for questions.

NOTES

Show Don't Tell

Writing is a collection of words that are born the day they are written and live for as long as the document that contains them is available. They become, "Jane says," with no deceased date if they are preserved in print.

It is different when we speak; the words are short lived, for that moment only, and are often forgotten within minutes. Often, spoken words are recalled incorrectly and then misinterpreted to twist the speaker's meaning. Even when someone records them, and quotes them correctly, later they use terms like, "Jane said whatever she said." They are for that moment in time.

Because words in print can endure long after we are gone and may be passed on for generations, it is important that we choose them carefully, making sure we require them to convey the meaning we intend.

What to write for the second lesson? Wow, not being a teacher by training and certainly without special expertise in English or Grammar, one may ask, "What can this guy share with me?" I am not sure either, and I don't have a detailed lesson plan. I just intend to provide a few hints of things that have helped me. I will get sidetracked from time-to-time, and share a reason or two for how I feel about a particular lesson. Notice that I didn't use the term,

"I may get sidetracked." I know I will, so why pretend that I may not. I am a person who loves to read something that is accurate, informative, entertaining, that moves me emotionally, and that generally leaves me feeling a little bit better.

Show, don't tell. This is one of my pet peeves and will cause me to put down what I am reading in an instant. This is one of the basic rules of writing. We want our reader to feel what we are writing, to be able to go there with us, to see what we see, to hear what we hear, to recall specific tastes or smells. When the reader is in the scene with us, his connection to what we are writing is instant and gratifying.

Example from where I grew up:

Often, on Sunday afternoons we stopped at the local ice cream store and then drove around until we passed a billboard with a cow that was always swinging its tail and sticking its tongue out. Mother always reminded us when we approached it to be sure we children didn't miss it. We always got a kick out of seeing it.

The previous is a true and informative statement, kind of boring, and not really entertaining. Consider:

Sunday afternoon we stopped at Tom's Dairy Freeze. Daddy and Mother always chose hard ice cream that had to be hand scooped, him black walnut and her lemon. Patsy and I would run to the window and stand peering in watching Tom's lanky fingers holding the tender cone as he swirled a soft white mound of ice cream neatly on top of her cone, and then doing the same for me, except in chocolate.

Patsy and I pressed our feet against the front seat to limit the rocking motion that threatened to knock our ice cream off our cones as Daddy backed the Ford onto Wilson Avenue, bouncing us around as we stopped abruptly. The car let out a grinding sound underneath our feet as he pulled the gearshift lever down, throwing us back against the seat as it lurched forward carrying us to our next destination.

There was not much conversation for the next few minutes as we all licked our cold treats. By the time we had turned onto Craft Highway and passed the icehouse, Daddy and I had finished ours, while Patsy and Mother were just getting to the hard shell of their cones.

"Y'all look, Dixie Dairies is on the left," Mother said as Daddy stopped the car at the red light. My cousin, Jimmy, was not working today. It was Sunday, and milk could be pasteurized another day.

We were always happy when the light was red because we could gawk just a little longer at the faithful old cow, always there, ten feet tall, fifteen feet in the air, mechanically swatting flies with her tail, and poking her tongue in and out at us. The car shivered forward as the light turned green, and we all craned our necks to see a little longer as Daddy pulled away, continuing on our humble family adventure.

I hope you see the difference in the two versions of the same story, and you understand the value of the latter. There are times to tell in a story, if there is a need to move past some unimportant but relevant facts, but more often, it is preferable to let the reader feel what the writer feels.

A few ingredients required for showing the reader what is happening:

1) Use dialog, pleasant or emotional conversation clearly lets the reader know how the characters feel.

2) Include descriptions that we can relate to our five senses, seeing, hearing, smelling, tasting, and feeling. If the reader can smell the hickory flavor in the smoke that is burning his eyes, he relates to the scene better.

3) Include lots of good description, a lot more than the bare facts.

4) Be specific, no fuzzy descriptions here. Instead of the car, call it a Ford or call the ice cream shop Tom's Dairy Freeze. Describe Tom's lanky fingers gently holding the crispy cone, maybe your mouth watering in anticipation.

Think of how you remember your own father when you were a child. How did you feel when you crawled up in his lap? Do you remember his ticklish facial stubble, the smell of his after shave, or maybe just the smell of his sweat? Tell how his huge but gentle arms surrounded you and provided a cocoon of protection from all would-be attackers.

For more information, go to google.com and type "show don't tell" and you will see many links to expand on what I say.

NOTES

Be Prepared

Because I had a few organizational skills, a little technical ability, and there was no one else better qualified available, I was assigned the task of leading a group of young graduate engineers. We were designing a system and purchasing the instruments required to control a new chemical plant to be built in another state.

After somehow successfully stumbling through that project, my boss, L. D. Pee, suggested, "Before your next salary evaluation, it would be good if you took some classes to improve your management skills." Until then, I had completed exactly nine quarter hours of college.

I signed up for Management 101 at the University of South Alabama.

"The first rule for success in business," Tommy Michael, the class instructor, said the first day of class, "Is to get to know the Siamese Twins of management."

I learned that the only thing these twins require is, to "Develop a Plan" and then "Control to the Plan." They require managers to follow their plan closely, maybe with a few minor adjustments as situations change.

So, I am thinking about following that rule very loosely to develop a basic writing lesson plan. I have been working on the plan, and hopefully I will have it developed fully before we get to the end. Right now, here goes:

An important rule a Boy Scout learns is to, "Be Prepared."

My goal is to pass to you a few hints that can help with any writing you may want to undertake. Some of you may have a book inside you; others may have a story or two that you want to tell, whether it is a true rendition of your life or of someone else's. You may want to write an instruction manual to teach skills that you have conquered.

You may have been reluctant to put your thoughts on paper. If you have, you may not feel free to share them with others. Both apprehensions are valid. The fear of rejection, for what we feel inside, is probably one of the greatest fears we have.

Let me assure you that many of us live with those fears all the time. It used to cripple me. I would sit in a room of people and listen intently; never joining in a conversation, because of the fear that others would laugh at me, or tell me that was a stupid comment. The only time I spoke was when I was with only one other person. and that person had to be someone I trusted.

Mr. Blake, a teacher at Vigor High School, used to impart his wisdom to us as he monitored the line of students waiting for lunch. One day he said, "If you are in a room full of people, and you sit there saying nothing, others may look at you and think you are pretty dumb. If you open your mouth and speak, you remove any doubt."

Even after I married Carolyn, I didn't share many of my thoughts with her. During those days, my Daddy was my most trusted friend. I would talk on the phone with him every evening, and Carolyn would sit close by and listen in, so she could learn what was going on deep down inside me. Now, she is my most trusted friend.

Here are a few hints for Lesson 3:

We all have good ideas that come to mind. We would like to write about them when we get somewhere more suitable. When we get to that convenient place and sit down to write, our mind goes blank. We can't recall it, can't bring it back to mind, no matter how hard we try. What to do?

1) Always have a piece of paper and pencil with you to jot down quick reminders so that you can recall your thoughts later when you have time.

2) I always have a pen & paper in my pants pocket. Some of my notes get to looking pretty ratty, and coupled with my poor cursive writing skills, I often have difficulty deciphering what I wrote, but I usually can summon up the original thought.

3) I almost always have my trusty iPhone with me. With it, I can use the notes feature to write the thought, or I can speak directly into it using the built-in voice recorder, especially if I am driving. It functions just like a tape recorder.

4) I suspect that some of you may have an iPad or another electronic writing device that you use, and it too would be a wonderful tool for quick notes.

5) There are all sorts of applications available for our electronic devices that can become useful tools, but I still prefer a plain ole piece of paper.

6) You are on your own on this one; but I seem to get a lot of inspiration during church, while the preacher

is delivering his sermon. I always have clean paper in my Bible, and if something the preacher says inspires me, I write it down. A side benefit is how quickly the service moves, while you are writing. A second benefit is others may believe you are recording the preacher's inspirational message. Sometimes, I am.

7) I have notebooks filled with thoughts and ideas that I have never shared with anyone else. Most of them are incomplete thoughts, but others reveal who I am, and who has influenced my life. I have shared some of them in this book.

Remember, God will bless your effort.

NOTES

Fiction Writing 1

How about a few tips for writing that story that lives only in "your" mind? The story is not true, the events didn't happen, the people never lived, but we all know the story, the events, and the people. If we write a story from the heart about people who struggle with problems, who are always trying to succeed, but continuously falling short, we will be writing about real life.

We could choose a person we know and write their biography, but if we do, we are limited to the facts. We can't deviate from the truth.

Fiction is different. We make up characters that are mixtures of people we know. Our first character is the protagonist, the star of our story. The next character is the antagonist, the one who is a thorn in the side of the protagonist. Then we add other characters to our story, not too many, because they get too difficult to keep up with.

Let's start with the protagonist and give him some good character traits, but then we are required by the unwritten laws of good fiction writing, to sprinkle in enough bad traits to cause him to be both lovable and despicable.

We have to do the same thing for all our other characters. Remember, even the worst antagonist, who is filled with evil traits, has some good character traits. He could be a murderer, but he supports programs that help at risk kids.

In the next few lessons, I will pass along a few tricks to help you develop your story.

When you notice a situation, you are in and say to yourself, "This could be part of a story," write down details, or keep a recorder handy to capture your thoughts.

Examples:

- I noticed the minute screams that were given off by some damp wood that I had just lit. It could remind you of something from the past.
- I walked out to get my paper one morning before daylight, and heard the soft rumbling of a garage door from a neighbor who doesn't ever acknowledge me. It could become part of a mysterious person in a story.
- I drove over the affectionately called "Dolly Parton" bridge that crosses the Mobile, Alabama river delta one morning. The car rose through a cloud and emerged on top. It was eerie looking down on the cotton white cloud underneath me. It reminded me of flying high above the clouds in an airplane, and then descending through it.

Note: *The bridge that we locals affectionately refer to as the "Dolly Parton" bridge, is named after a former director of the Army Corps of Engineers, General W. K. Wilson Jr. However, when one approaches the bridge from the south on I-65, It is easy to see why it earned the popular nickname.*

- As I descended through the clouds, the fog surrounding the car again, I wanted to slow down or stop, but images of that 18-wheeler I had just passed, loomed in my mind. What a relief for the fog to melt away as I continued across the lower bridges of the delta.

- The barren treetops pierced the fog that lay low between the bridges covering the rivers that I know are there. London fog is what it reminded me of.
- The sun streamed through the leafless tree branches breaking the haze of the fog like a smoke-filled area from a smoldering fire. The sun breaking through occasionally and warming the bare spots.

I could go on, but you get the idea.

Start a notebook to hold your details, break it into three sections. I will tell you what to keep in the other two sections in the next lesson.

Thanks for reading my thoughts.

NOTES

Fiction Writing 2

In the previous lesson, I asked you to start a notebook and divide it into three sections.

Section-1: Record scene details; situations that you find yourself in that may be the beginning of a fictional scene in a story or book that you are writing.

In this lesson, add the next two sections:

Section-2: Record names. When you see or hear a name that intrigues you and you say to yourself, "That could be a name that I would use in my story," write it down.

Some names I have on my list:

- Emily Mattison – I plan to use this name for a child in a novel I am writing
- Becky – I plan to use this name to be my protagonists' first love
- Lucy – I plan to use this as the name of my protagonists' final love
- I am looking for a name for a fictional well-known senator who has lived a hypocritical life, something that sounds good but that is synonymous with the devil. One name I am considering is Samael, Angel of Death or Prince of Demons. It wouldn't work if he was Jewish because most of the Jewish faith would understand, but here in south Alabama, some would

think that his mother and dad just decided to use a different spelling. They have probably called him Sam all his life. In the end, the name is perfectly suited for him.

Other names I have on my list:
* Molly
* Hattie
* Conrad
* Ival
* Lucius
* Harley
* Sydney
* Rose

Section-3: Record character details. List things that make an individual stand out to you. Some of my details are:

* Cigar smoking, deep crusty voice. I wonder if his vocal cords have been damaged because of his smoking.

* I remember my next-door neighbor as very smart. A fellow second grader, she could spell a lot more words than me. I was wowed when she spelled hippopotamus. I didn't have a clue. She didn't tout her skills in any way that made me feel insecure.

* Mr. Rhoades could eat an apple and chew tobacco at the same time. It was kind of sickening watching him. He had no manners, he had a spit cup on his desk, and another one he kept on the seat of his car. It was always scary riding with him, hoping that thing didn't turn over when he made a left turn.

Expand your lists as much as you like and refer to them when you need inspiration.

Continue to build your personal database of thoughts and ideas to draw from as you develop your stories.

NOTES

The Right Word 1

As I write this, my mind is bouncing from one thought to another. There are so many ideas and so many words, but readers will tolerate a limited quantity of each at any one time. Today, let's focus on the importance of using the "Right Word."

In order to convey our thoughts perfectly leaving no question as to our intended meaning, we must choose the right word.

How do you learn to use the right word?

It's not that hard. Start with what you already know. You have a lifetime of word gathering in you. The older you are, the more you have heard, and the more you have used.

Young children have fewer words to draw from. They have been spoken to by adults who butcher the English language to make the words easier and more fun. They hear words like peep-pie, koochey-koo, bye-bye, da-da, ma-ma, outside, and the most dreaded, "No!"

School age children have more words and college students know even more words. Adults and career professionals continue building their library. We all should be on the alert for words that we are not very familiar with and continue adding them to our inventory.

Get a good dictionary, keep it close, and use it. I like a hardback that will stay open to the page I am looking at. You may find a good one at a flea market or a used bookstore for only a few bucks. Although, most smart phones allow you to look up a word on-line with instant access from anywhere, I still like to exercise my own alphabetical search capability and look directly at printed words. When to use a dictionary? When you read or hear someone speak a word that you are not sure of the meaning, jot it down, and look it up when you have time.

Make a list of words that you have recently learned and look for opportunities to use them. Here are a few from my list:

- Stodge: Dull & uninspiring
- Petulant: Childishly sulky or bad tempered, a petulant shake of the head
- Prig-Self: Righteous moralistic person who behaves as if superior to others
- Ineffable: Words cannot describe, too great or extreme to be expressed or described in words, not to be uttered
- Efficacy: The ability to produce a desired or intended result
- Bethlehem: Place where Jesus was born. We are to be a *Bethlehem*, a place for Jesus to be a born into
- Censorious: Highly critical of others
- Obtuseness: Slow to understand
- Caprice: A sudden & unaccountable change in mood or behavior
- Lodestar: Guiding light or principal

- Quaver: Shake or tremble in speaking, *Tommy's voice didn't quaver, he just struggled to get all the syllables out.*
- Crucible: A place or occasion of severe test (like crucify)
- Ascetic: Severe self-discipline
- Antipodes: The direct opposite of something
- Liminal: 1. Of or relating to a sensory threshold, 2. Barely perceptible, 3. Of, relating to, or being an intermediate state, phase, or condition; in-between, transitional
- Hirple: Walk with a limp (lamely), to limp, hobble,
- Innocency: Freedom from guilt or sin through being unacquainted with evil: blamelessness, faultlessness, guiltlessness, impeccability, innocence
- Malevolent: Having a wish or showing a wish to do evil to others, malicious or spiteful

The following short story illustrates how we learn new words:

When our girls were young, Carolyn and I moved to Pensacola, and bought a small house in Warrington, close to my work. We befriended the young newlywed couple who lived next door, and after a couple of years they had their first child.

The husband managed an Eckerd's drug store, one of a chain that stayed open until 8:00 every night, and he was required to be there most nights until closing.

Almost every afternoon, Sandy, the wife, came over and visited with my wife, Carolyn; partly to get some help, and maybe to gain some wisdom about raising her son, but probably more important to her was to have some adult company. Our girls entertained Matthew and we three adults enjoyed visiting.

It was during one of these vespertine visits that Matthew spoke his first word. We were all speechless as we realized what he had just said. What did he say? Da-Da, Ma-Ma? No. No, the first word that Matthew spoke was the one he had heard repeated more than any other during his young life. "Wayne."

American English is a beautiful language and we should seek to express its beauty at every opportunity.

More on selecting the right word will be continued in later lessons.

NOTES

The Right Word 2

In the previous lesson, I talked about the importance of having a good dictionary, so that we fully understand the meaning of the words we write. There are not nearly enough words in my head to provide instant revelation of the exact word I should select for any given situation. Because of my background and education, I have words from certain groupings that I understand.

I work in an engineering office, so I understand such words as design, CAD, beams, supports, milliamps, scheduling, estimating, cost analysis, terminations, schematics, plans, isometrics, blueprints, etc. When I write proposals, I have a lot of words that I can use to ensure that project managers understand what I plan to do.

I also like to work on cars, so I understand how engines work with their pistons, crankshafts, cams, etc.

I fish some, so I understand a little about rods, reels, grubs, corks, fishing line, hooks, nets, lead weights, and Mississippi shiners.

I could go on and on pointing out words for areas that I know a little about. Even with my understanding of the various areas mentioned, I do not know or remember every word that may be available to convey my thoughts properly. That's where I turn to the second reference book that everyone should have.

Get a Good Synonym Finder and reference it often. I picked mine up at the local flea market. "The Synonym Finder" by J.I. Rodale and Staff, copyright 1961 sixth printing—March 1967. It is hardback also and I leave it open on my desk when I write, always ready to come to my aid. My copy came with a short hand-written note that reads, "To Ann Dickson Newman—so that she may speak and write with correctness, accuracy, and precision. Love, Papa – April 18, 1970." I read that note often. I am always touched that someone cared enough about another person to purchase such a thoughtful tool.

You can find an inexpensive thesaurus almost anywhere, probably even at the dollar store. In addition, most word processing software has a built-in thesaurus, be quick to use it.

Someone may ask why we would want to use words we don't already know the meaning. Well, we should always be open to expanding our vocabulary. We all know and understand literally thousands of words when we read them. If we don't know the exact meaning, we can deduce the meaning depending on the context and other words in a sentence. However, when we write, we must be sure we are writing our words correctly. There can be no question, or our readers will catch them in a heartbeat. It goes to the integrity of our writing, where I intended for integrity in this sentence to capture its double meaning, whole and honest.

What did you think of my use of the word vespertine in the short story in *The Right Word 1* lesson? It was during one of these vespertine visits that Matthew spoke his first word.

I could have written "evening," but I had already used enough words to indicate that we met sometime in between the afternoon to late night, and I like to add a little touch of elegance. I could have replaced elegance in the previous sentence with variety, style, panache, or finesse.

We can use the synonym finder to help us avoid overuse of certain words. To me, unless there is a specific reason for emphasis, we should never use the same word more than once in a sentence, and preferably not more than once in a single paragraph. If there is a reason to repeat a word several times during an article, look for other words that mean something similar, or that provide a more exact meaning each time it is written.

When I opened my synonym finder today, the note was between pages 828 and 829 and the word my eye went to was oppose. Most of us understand what oppose means so let's see.

Dictionary Definition of Verb Oppose:

1. Disapprove of and attempt to prevent, especially by argument: *Those who oppose capital punishment*

2. Actively resist or refuse to comply with (a person or a system).

Synonyms for Oppose: (just a few)

- Counterbalance, like when we sit on a seesaw, the two opposing forces balance in such a way that we can rise up and down without much exertion

- Resist, can mean to push back against an aggressor, or run against as in opponents in an election

- Withstand, contest, strive, contend, struggle, counteract, repulse, repel, make a stand against, confront, face, fight, war, battle, joust, clash, scuffle, wrestle, attack, assault, grapple with

- Contradict, defy, withstand, antagonize, obstruct, check, thwart, block, interdict, embargo, hinder, impede, veto, oppugn, resist, restrain, inhibit, constrain, interfere, bar, barricade, prohibit, foil, cross, confound, traverse, repel, frustrate, recalcitrate, repulse, protest

Most of us understand the meaning of nearly all the above synonyms, and with so many to choose from, we should never write the word oppose multiple times in any article. Think about the context of your idea and select other words that convey an accurate meaning to your audience. Consider the following:

Best friends Jim and Joe signed up as members of the same wrestling team, but during practice the coach lined them up against each other on opposing teams. It was not long before they lay on the mat, each struggling to overpower the other.

At first when you start looking up words in a thesaurus, your articles may not read as well as you would like, but soon with a little practice and encouragement, you will be selecting with the best of them.

We will continue Choosing the Right Word in the next lesson.

NOTES

The Right Word 3

How important is the right word?

Consider the young engineer that I worked with years ago. Ching Yi and her husband were from Taiwan. They had moved to the United States, earned their degrees, and found engineering jobs in Mobile. One day, one of our Louisiana Cajuns, an LSU graduate, was picking at her the way a lot of young American men do with each other.

Ching Yi was getting frustrated with not understanding why he was saying the things he was. Mister Fix-It, me, stepped in and said simply, "Do not take Jason seriously; he is just pulling your leg."

She quickly responded, "No, he never touched me."

I immediately realized that even though I knew what I was saying, Ching Yi did not. Even though she was fluent in English and had better grammatical skills than me, she didn't understand the street language of south Alabama.

I had to modify my comment to her, and explain that he was joking, and was trying to help her fit in.

<u>Depute:</u>

One client sent an email to me and asked me to depute one of our engineers to come up and check out a problem. I had no clue what he was asking me to do, but after a quick check of the dictionary, I discovered he was saying that he wanted me to deputize someone and get them to take care of his problem. He could have asked me to authorize, or to simply send someone to check out his problem.

Much Obliged:

My dad often said, "Much obliged." It was only two words, but they define the very heart of this quiet Mississippi native who was thankful for everything that anyone had ever done for him. He never took anything for granted, and he knew that everything that anyone did for him, cost them something.

He could just as easily have said, "Thank you," but that may not have made such a lasting impression on a son who learned from him the basics of living, the necessity for working, and the importance of giving thanks to those who do for me.

Tailgating:

A client and I had traveled to Denham Springs, Louisiana for meetings and while we were there, some of the people, who were LSU fans invited him to come to one of their tailgating parties at Tiger stadium. Being from India, he listened quietly, smiling occasionally, and nodding as if he understood.

When we started back to Mobile, with a planned side trip through New Orleans to go to one of the international food warehouses, he asked me what is this tailgating that they were talking about? I explained that at ballgames fans would meet and set up a place to picnic and fellowship with friends. They have a lot of good food and use the time to encourage each other about the upcoming game.

He was satisfied with my explanation commenting that he now understood what they were talking about. It was not long before we turned onto the Pontchartrain causeway. The first sign we saw read, "NO TAILGATING." My work was not done.

The Right Word

Consider: Webster's first dictionary, printed in the early 1800's, contained about 70,000 words. There are probably more than a million variations of words available to us now.

I read that William Shakespeare used 29,066 different words in all his published works, including proper names, to pen his celebrated stories. (The American Heritage Dictionary, Second College Edition)

In writing, it is better if we choose the best word to convey the exact meaning of what we want our readers to understand.

NOTES

Check it Meticulously

Consider a young man fresh out of work, a wife, three children, and needing to find employment soon, real soon.

I read about a job opening for a mechanic at Toomey Equipment, a local tractor and farm implement supply company.

Let me go back a bit. I learned to fix things around the house and on cars working alongside my daddy, either in the rental apartments he purchased to supplement the family income, or in the garage behind our house in Alabama Village.

I improved my skills during my high school years because the cars I drove needed a lot of tender loving care to keep them running, especially after the way I treated them.

After high school, I worked for three years as a pipefitter helper at International Paper Company in Mobile, and then served a four-year apprenticeship with the Naval Air Station in Pensacola. I worked three more years as an aircraft electrician repairing electrical systems on various U. S. Navy aircraft, both jets and propeller driven planes. I loved that job but got caught in a presidential campaign promise to shrink the size of government.

Although the navy offered me my old job back, Carolyn and I decided to bring our family home to Mobile. I accepted a job with Warrior and Gulf Navigation in Chickasaw repairing diesel engines, and other mechanical equipment on 85-foot-long tugboats. After working there for only eleven months, I knew that was not the job for me, so I resigned.

I tried my hand at selling tires and automobile services for another eleven months with Ira Lewis Sr. in Saraland, Alabama, until it was established that sales is another skill that had eluded me. Another resignation and I am back to the start of this story.

How hard could it be to fix tractors and farm equipment?

I had read a book on how to write a resume to get an interview and because this was the third job I was seeking in as many years, I updated mine. At the end I listed some of my positive character traits, the final one, "I am very thourough."

I was so proud of that resume and the person I would be working for was equally impressed. We talked about the job a long time and we wanted to work it out but could not agree on a salary. Naturally I wanted more than he was authorized to pay.

As we finished up, he promised to try and get the amount of money I needed, and that he would be back in touch. As I exited the building, a lady handed me my resume without saying a word. As I got in my car, I noticed that she had circled one word on my resume, "thourough" as if to say, "Not as much as you think."

In an effort to showcase my skills, I overlooked one little detail that belied the very point that I was trying to prove.

Did you catch it? If I had, I may still be a tractor mechanic.

NOTES

CONCLUSION

I believe we should live as if today will be our last, but we should plan as if we will live to be a hundred. Somewhere in between is reality.

One day, likely when we least expect it, God will give the nod to one of his angels, saying, "Go get Wayne Brady or <insert your name>, tell him I have prepared a home for him, and I want to share dinner with him today."

After we are seated at the table, God will say something like, "Dear son, I am so happy to see you. I love you, and I am delighted to have you here. You are the perfect addition to our wonderful home."

Am I a good and faithful servant? No, but our Father says, "Yes."

Do you understand this promise? Have you received it for yourself? If not, it is easy and free to all who ask. Simply give your heart to God, place your faith and trust in His son, Jesus. Believe that Jesus is who He said He is and ask Him to come into your heart. Then you will be born again as a new person, clean throughout, with a new outlook and high expectations.

Will you be perfect? No, but in God's eyes, Yes.

Will victory be easy? Sometimes, but other times, it may be very difficult. Life will continue to try and weigh you down. The neat thing is, God will always be with you, encouraging you to do what is right. The easier we accept His guidance, the less pain we will feel. If we balk openly, He will be more stern with us. He will get our attention!

I pray you have enjoyed reading these stories and that you have been encouraged in your walk with God, family, and friends. Welcome to my world.

Feel free to contact me for support and feedback.

Your Friend in Jesus Christ,

Wayne Brady

NOTES

ACKNOWLEDGMENTS

Thank You, God for inspiring me, and for putting people in my life to teach and encourage me. The realization that You love me and have revealed Yourself to me is awesome. Thank You for allowing me to write these words as if they are my own. Thank You for reminding me of each incident and person I have shared through these stories. You are truly a loving Father.

Thank you, Carolyn Brady, my wife, the most wonderful and beautiful person I know. You have been my strength and greatest encourager for more than half a century. I could never have finished this without you.

Thank you Will Headrick, Norma Vaughn Danzey, Louise Davis, and Aleta Davis. As fellow members of the Misfits Writing group, each of you have been so encouraging, both in reviewing my writing and teaching me how to press on to publication. You all are truly a blessing to me.

Thank you, J. Steve Biggs, longtime friend, schoolmate, and fellow author, for reviewing my book and offering your insight. Your attention to detail offered many helpful suggestions.

Thank you, Phil and Julia Guinn my most recent best friends. Your encouragement, knowledge of writing, feedback and desire to see me succeed has boosted my confidence in this work.

Special thanks to the Southern Christian Writers Conference. Your annual event is like a revival for writers. Thank you, David and Joanne Sloan, Cheryl Sloan Wray, and Sammie Jo Floyd Barstow for your personal touch in my life.

ABOUT THE AUTHOR

WAYNE BRADY

Wow, still going after seven decades, a work in progress, too young to give up, too old to accept failure. I have learned a few valuable lessons through my experiences that I have shared with you.

I am a husband, married to the same woman for more than five decades, a father of three, and a grandfather of five.

A country boy who moved from a small Mississippi community where we could not see the next house on the highway, to a heavily populated and growing metropolitan area with kids everywhere. It was wonderful growing up in Prichard Alabama, attending Mobile County public schools, and graduating with nearly 450 other likeminded classmates.

My daddy told me that if I learned a trade, I would always be able to find work. Growing up in the depression, that was very important to him. So, I listened. I learned the electrical trade and worked 24 years maintaining equipment to keep industrial plants operating. Because I knew how to make things work, I discovered an opportunity with a large engineering company where I helped young engineers learn to put theory into practical use.

It soon became apparent, I had to upgrade my skills. I had to go back to school. At the age of 52, I earned an associates degree from Pensacola Junior College, and then graduated magna cum laude with a bachelor's degree from The University of Alabama. Little did I know how important learning would become. It's more than a piece of paper, it's an addition to my life that keeps me viable.

I have passed the age where I have earned the right to relax and enjoy my twilight years, I intend to do just that. But it won't be by sitting and doing nothing. No, I intend to keep actively working, some with industry, working on projects around home, but more importantly by sharing through words that God has given me.

Please receive everything I write with the humble spirit God gave to me. I offer it in Love for You and in praise of My Lord and Savior Jesus Christ.

Made in the USA
Columbia, SC
26 November 2021